Past Times

(Children's Games By: Pieter Bruegel)

Sports and Games of Medieval Europe

By: Jeffrey S. Johnston

Living History Publications

First Printing: 2016

ISBN: 978-0-9948501-3-3

Dedicated to Penny Bateson who helped much in editing this book, she never got to see the finished product, but I hope she would be proud of what was accomplished. And thank you to Beth who picked where Penny left off and helped me finish this.

Thanks also go out to Faye, who not only tolerated my obsession with medieval games, but encouraged me on this crazy journey to write this book and start the Past Times series. Without her love and support this book, and all others in the Past Times series would not never have been more than just a passing idea.

Contents

Introduction

"You can discover more about a person in an hour of play than in a year of conversation."
Plato

For several years I have been a member of the Society for Creative Anachronisms and even before that I had considerable interest in the medieval era. One thing I have discovered in researching this time period is that the history of games is an area that is usually overlooked. Often people will outright state that the pastimes of your average medieval person were dancing, music, and… that's about it. This romanticized version of medieval life is all well and good but overlooks the rich variety of games played throughout the ages.

Historians often downplay the importance of games. In fact if you look at the vast amounts of history books you will be hard pressed to find many historical sports books that aren't statistics of modern games. Those that do exist are generally placed in the sports section of the library and not the history section, so it is clear that serious study of the history of sports is not even generally considered in the study of history at all.

It is my personal belief, however, that if you look at how a society plays you will find more about them than looking at any other single aspect of their culture. By overlooking sports, games, toys, and other leisure activities while researching a past culture, you are left with only a partial view of its people. Only the examination of a cultures pastimes can you get a clear grasp of history. In games people are at their best and worst. Views on cheating in games, can for example, shed light on views of dishonesty within the community and their culture as a whole. Researching gambling can illuminate the value of goods. The study of games is not just a fun aspect of history, but shows us our ancestors as human, something many branches of historical study fails to do.

In the past, a common belief was that the playing of games was one of the defining characteristics of humanity. This, however, falls apart when one studies the animal kingdom. It seems almost all animals have some level of play during their development. To me, this indicates that the playing of games is more primal than we have previously believed, and thus more important than we have claimed it to be. Our culture may place an inordinate amount of importance on the playing of games, but we are not unique in that.

The very fact that we call those that excel at a given sport "heroes" shows the importance humanity places on prowess in games. You could argue that this is just modern culture demonstrating their cult of the famous, worshiping those who aren't really worthy but rather glamorous. However, it's not just modern culture that has worshiped sporting prowess. The great Gaelic hero Sétanta was first noticed by the fact that he single headedly beat an entire group of boys at what appears to be a football game, then when they try to beat him up for interfering, he bests them all at wrestling. After this, he fought off a hound, killing it with a hurley ball, of all things, which the Lord Chulainn had left on guard forgetting Sétanta was coming over. This dead granted him his mythic name of *Cú Chulainn*. Obviously sports played a rather large part in the young life of legendary Cú Chulainn.

Many people suppose that playing of games developed as a way to keep our body in shape and prepare us for battle and/or the hunt. When you examine play, however, you realize this theory doesn't really hold up. During play, precious resources are often cast aside, and often injury results. This is true in the playing of sports in modern culture, and in play in the animal kingdom. If playing games developed as a means of survival and to stay fit, then injuring oneself in that pursuit, or casting aside precious resources seems counterproductive. Many psychologists are beginning to believe that play does more for mental development than it does for muscular development. So now, maybe finally, the battle of the ages between the nerds and the jocks can finally come to terms and agree that they are both exercising their intellectual muscles, just in different forms.

Many games did develop out of martial training. Hop scotch, for instance, was said to have originated from a training regimen the Roman's used in which they would essentially play bouts of hop scotch in full armour. It is believed that children began imitating this and modifying it to be the game we know today. Other cases, such as tug of war and other feats of strength, were probably also partially martial in origin.

Regardless of origin, when all is said and done, people play games to have fun. This is the entire point of this book, to have fun playing games. With this book, I hope to introduce some of the best of medieval fun and games, and reintroduce some to old favourites that some people may not have known were medieval in origin. This is by no means a complete list of all the games ever played in Medieval Europe, but rather a brief overview of some of my personal favourite games. The book is intended to be not just a list of games with their historical background, but also as a manual on how to play the games.

By all means get some friends together for a game night and recreate some medieval gaming fun.

Board Games

"The game of chess is not merely an idle amusement. Several very valuable qualities of the mind, useful in the course of human life, are to be acquired or strengthened by it, so as to become habits, ready on all occasions. For life is a kind of chess, in which we have often points to gain, and competitors or adversaries to contend with, and in which there is a cast of variety of good and evil events, that are, in some degree, the effects of prudence or the want of it. By playing at chess, then, we may learn."

Benjamin Franklin

Board games have a rich and fascinating history in medieval times. The Vikings actually listed skills at board games as one of the nine skills all nobles should know (Gordon, 1981). Games such as Chess and Backgammon are often called a "Kings Game" but several board games have been called that throughout the ages.

Generally in medieval times board games, much like today, were used as a method to pass time on days where the weather was too bad outside. Often various board games have also been used to pass time long sea voyages. While many games seem impractical to play on a rocking ship, pegs could often be used for the men and the boards would have holes drilled to fit the pegs into. Basically board games were just something to keep the mind active during idle times. Most have a highly strategic aspect and require concentration and skill to win.

Medieval board games are easy to reproduce and lots of fun to play.

Rithmomachia

Rithmomachia, or the Philosophers Game is a complex mathematical game not for the faint of heart. It has often been reputed that the game was invented by the great mathematician and philosopher Pythagoras. However there is no real evidence of this, although certainly without the works of Pythagoras and others of his stature the game would not be possible.

It is certainly evident that its popularity in the 11th and 12th centuries in monastic schools throughout Germany and France was epic. As early as 1030 there were competitions between schools in Rithmomachia, notably one between Würzburg and Worms, two schools well known for their mathematical prowess. Some think a monk named Asilo created the game specifically for this competition based on the work of Boethius in order to teach his mathematical theories (Mebben). Like so many other games, the real origins of Rithomachia have been lost.

Rithmomachia is a two player game, generally one plays white the other black. The board is a sixteen by eight grid. The pieces are complex, but they break down to four basic types, Rounds, Squares, Triangles and Pyramids. Pyramids are not an individual piece exactly, but rather a stack made up of several other pieces they are stacked with the highest value piece on the bottom and the lowest on the top. The game is unbalanced, but fans of the game are divided as to which side has an actual advantage.

How to Win:

Before beginning the players must agree on victory conditions. There are several methods of victory that fit into two basic catagories, Common Victories and Proper Victories.

Common Victories:

- The Victory of Body: Taking a set number of the opponents pieces.

- The Victory of Assets: To take a set value of the opponents pieces.

- The Victory of Procedes: To take a set number of digits for example you could agree that whoever takes the 9 25 and 81 pieces wins.

Proper Victories:

In proper victories the object is to take the opponents pyramid then form an arithmetic, geometric or harmonic progression in the opponents side of the board.

- The Mediocre Victory: Achieving a single progression using at least three pieces.

- The Great Victory: Achieving two progressions at once using at least four pieces. In this case two pieces could fit into two separate progressions for example 5 10 15 25 would work as 5 10 15 is an arithmatic progression of 5s and 5 15 25 is an arithmatic progression of 10s. Of course both progressions aren't required to be the same type you could have an arithmatic and a geometric.

- The Excellent Victory: Achieving three progressions using at least four pieces.

Pieces:

White pieces:

- Rounds 3, 5, 7, 9, 9, 25, and 81

- Triangles 12, 30, 56, 90, 16, 36, 64, and 100

- Squares 28, 66, 120, 49, 121, 225, and 361

- The white pyramid is made up of a Square 64,

Square 49, Triangle 36, Triangle 25, and a Round 16 for a value of 190

Black pieces:

- Rounds 2, 4, 6, 8, 16, 36, and 64

- Triangles 6, 20, 42, 72, 9, 25, and 81

- Squares 15, 45, 153, 25, 81, 169, and 289

- The black pyramid is made up of a Square 36, Square 25, Triangle 16, Triangle 9, Round 4, and a Round 1 for a value of 91

Board Set-Up:

A standard Rythmomachia board is an 8X16 grid, often checkered. It can be played by setting two chessboards side by side with one board as the white side and the other as the black side.

Black Side (Pyramid shown as P91)

25	81					169	289
15	45	25	20	42	49	P91	153
9	6	4	16	36	64	72	81
			2	4	6	8	

White Side (pyramid Shown as P190)

			9	7	5	3	
100	90	81	49	25	9	12	16
P190	120	64	56	30	36	66	28
361	225					121	49

Moves:

There are two types of moves in the game, regular and irregular. Regular moves requires the path be unobstructed, which means no men in their path, irregular can move regardless of anything it its path. Circles only move regularly, there are no valid irregular moves for circles, they can move one space diagonally. Triangles move two spaces horizontally or vertically for their regular moves, and like a rook in chess (two spaces horizontally or vertically then turn 90° in any direction and one move one space) for irregular moves. Square pieces move three spaces horizontally or vertically for regular moves and for irregular three horizontal or vertical moves and then a 90° turn in any direction and move one space.

Captures:

There are several ways to capture an opposing players pieces. A capture can take place either before or after a regular move:

- *The Encounter:* During a turn if an opponent's piece is within one regular move of your piece and it is of equivalent value you can capture that piece and take its place.

- *The Imprisonment:* If a piece has all possible regular moves blocked by an opponent's pieces that piece may be taken by the opponent.

- *The Ambush:* The ambush requires two capturing pieces to be within one regular move of the victim. If the sum, difference, product, or ratio of the two capturing pawns then one of the two pieces can capture the opponent pawn and take its place. Many variants only allow for the capture to take place if the two capturing pieces sums add up to the captured piece and ignores the ratio, difference, or product.

- *The Progression:* When a piece can be made up of part of an arithmetic, harmonic, or geometric progression with at least two opposing pieces that piece can be taken, assuming both opposing pieces are within one regular move of the victim. For example if a 20 and 15 were both within one move of 25 the 25 can be taken as they are part of an arithmetic progression by fives.

- *The Assault:* If a piece encounters an opponent in the same row, column or diagonal that has the number of unoccupied spaces between time equal to the product or ratio of the two numbers the opponents piece can be captured.

- *The Power:* When a number is equal to the power or roots of an opposing pawn it may be taken if it is within one regular move of said opposing pawn. For example if 3 is within one regular move of 81 the three can take the 81 because 3 is the fourth root of 81.

Pyramids can capture or be captured using either any one of the individual pieces, or the combined value of all remaining pieces.

It is not mandatory to capture a piece if it is possible, there may be strategic advantage to not capture a piece and as such a player may choose to leave it alone. (Thibault)

Tafl

Tafl is the Old Norse word for Table and thus is simply a Viking name for board games. The tafl series of games presented here are specific capture strategy games. The Viking Sagas go into great length about playing tafl games, but rarely do we see any rules, as such most tafl games have to be recreated from other sources. One thing to note about Tafl games is that the rules were never formalized, as such each region tended to have its own set of rules and layout options. The starting positions I will be given are more guidelines than hard and fast rules. Experiment with the start positions and general rules and see what works best for you.

In the rules used in this book, I state that to capture a king you need three surrounding men to capture him, however in most redactions it is assumed it takes four men. There is no evidence supporting either case in the Viking Sagas, however the three man take down rule allows for more balance in the game.

Hnefatafl

Hnefatafl is a Viking age game often referred to as "Kings Table". When someone wishes to play Tafl they are most likely referring to Hnefatafl.

There are countless mentions of hnefatafl in the Norse sagas, but unfortunately not a single recounting of how the game is actually played. As such the game has to be reconstructed from more modern variants of the game, which luckily are plentiful. Generally in the sagas hnefatafl is referred only to as tafl, but tafl is a whole range of games including chess called *skaktafl* and backgammon called *kvatrutafl* (Peterson, 2001). Leaving chess and backgammon out of the equation, for the purposes of this book I will refer to tafl games as variants of hnefatafl.

The best description of how to play tafl games comes from a diary by Linnaeus from 1732 that documented his visits to Lapland and the playing of a game called Tablut, a hnefatafl variant played on a 9X9 game board as shown below.

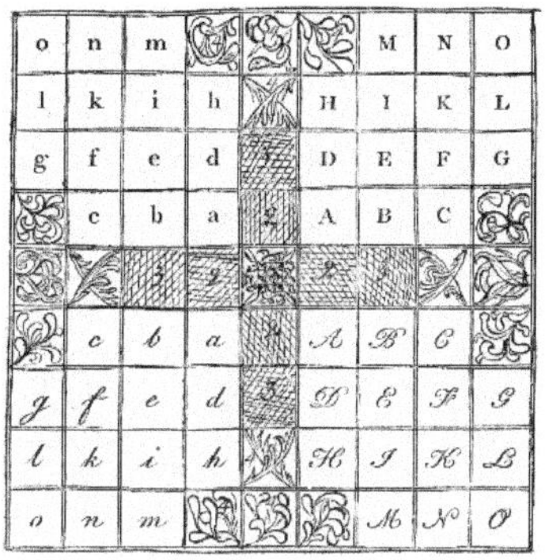

(Smith, 1811)

Linnaeus clearly lays out some rules that can be extrapolated to be used for hnefatafl and its variants. For the reconstructed rules I use I don't use Liunnaeus' rules exactly but a slightly modified version to help adjust for a strong bias for the defending team.

Hnefatafl is played on an 11X11 board and is laid out as shown. Where attackers are signified as "A" defenders as "D" and the king as "K".

X			A	A	A	A	A			X
				A						
A					D					A
A				D	D	D				A
A	A		D	D	K	D	D		A	A
A				D	D	D				A
A					D					A
X			A	A	A	A	A			X

Since the attackers are the ones making a move on the defenders they begin and turns alternate back and forth. All men can move in straight lines (no diagonal movement) for as many squares as they wish as long as it is uninterrupted by another player or a square they cannot land on.

The restricted squares are the centre square and the four corners are only for the king.

For the attackers the goal is to kill the king. For the defenders the goal is to escape, or more aptly get the king to any of the four corners (marked with X on the game board shown).

To make a kill two pieces must be on adjoining squares to the target piece. The only exception is the king, who requires three attackers to kill him. The reason for this is one Viking against another will be evenly matched, but throw a second man at him and he is quickly outmatched. The king however is the most powerful warrior in the area thus it two warriors against him and he can hold out, the third is what takes him out. In all cases a player can move into a position that would normally cause that pieces loss without losing the piece. In this case it takes a third man, the reason being if a single Viking surprises two other Vikings he will be able to hold out on the element of surprise, it would take a third man to kill him. Examples of valid kills are shown below.

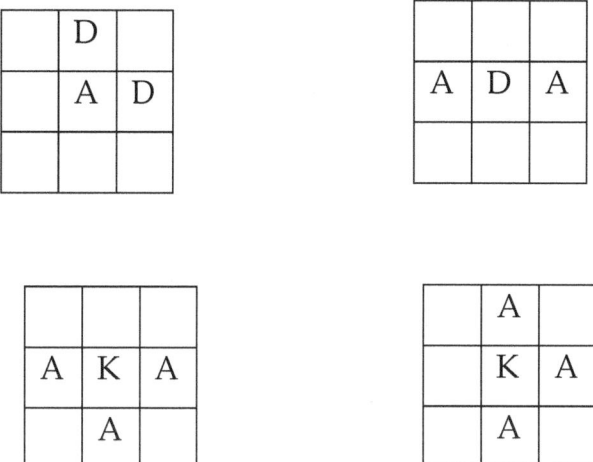

The following is NOT a valid kill as diagonal kills are not permitted.

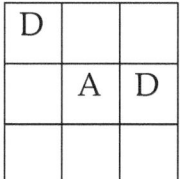

If you wished to add randomness to the game it could be played using dice to determine the maximum number of spaces a given man could move. There is no direct evidence that dice were used to play hnefatafl, however there is no direct evidence to suggest dice weren't used. Vikings were certainly familiar with dice and quite enjoyed them.

Alea Evangelii

Alea Evangelii (game of the gospels) is a hnefatafl variant that is played using essentially the same rules as hnefatafl, the only difference being how the board is set up. (Peterson, 2001)

1	2	3	4	5	6	7	8	9	10	11	12	13	14	15	16	17	18
X		A		A								A			A		X
A				A								A					A
					A		D		D		A						
A	A			A								A			A		A
					A				D				A				
				A				D		D				A			
					D			D		D		D			D		
				A			D		D	K	D		D			A	
					D			D		D		D			D		
				A				D		D				A			
					A				D				A				
					A				D				A				
A	A			A								A			A		A
					A		D		D		A						
A				A								A					A
X		A		A								A			A		X

Tawlbwrdd

Tawlbwrdd is a Welsh variant which is still a relatively commonly played variant of hnefatafl. Like Alea Evangelii it is played with the same rules and only the board varies.

X				D	D	D				X
				D		D				
					D					
					A					
D	D			A	A	A			D	D
D		D	A	A	K	A	A	D		D
D	D			A	A	A			D	D
					A					
					D					
				D		D				
X				D	D	D				X

Brandub

Brandub is an Irish variant. Again it is played with the same rules just a different board configuration.

X			A			X
			A			
			D			
A	A	D	K	D	A	A
			D			
			A			
X			A			X

Ard Ri

Ard Ri is the Scottish version.

X		A	A	A		X
			A			
A		D	D	D		A
A	A	D	K	D	A	A
A		D	D	D		A
			A			
X		A	A	A		X

Tablut

Tablut comes to us from Lapland or Sápmi and is the best documented form of hnefatafl. According to Linnaeus tablut is a game played on a 9X9 board with 25 pieces. (Smith, 1811)

X			A	A	A			X
				A				
				D				
A				D				A
A	A	D	D	K	D	D	A	A
A				D				A
				D				
				A				
X			A	A	A			X

Halatafl

Halatafl is more commonly known now as Fox and Geese and is reputed to have been a favorite game of Queen Victoria (Sackson, 1999). Although it is considered a relative of hnefatafl and the tafl family of games, the game play varies considerably. The ealiest mention of halatafl comes to us from the Grettis Saga which mentions the game several times.

The board layout and starting positions are as shown below:

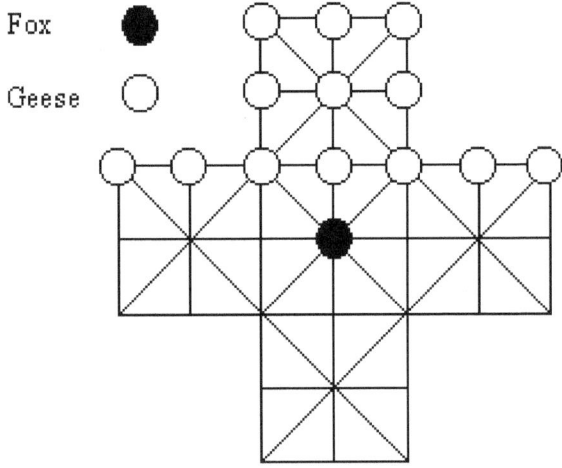

Each player takes turns moving, each piece can only move to one of the adjacent spots. Geese get the honour of moving first. The Fox can remove geese by jumping them as you do in checkers, repeated jumps are permitted. The game ends when the Geese have only three remaining pieces, this is a win for Fox, or when the Fox has no remaining legal moves, Geese win.

Like other tafl games it is an unbalanced game with a distinct advantage going to the Fox. This can be combatted by allowing for some extra Geese.

Morris

Nine Man Morris and its variants, also known as Merrels in France and Mills in Germany, are well known medieval board games. Morris boards can be found in stone work all over Europe from pre roman times right up to modern times (Berger, 2004).

The common varieties are three man morris, six man morris, nine man morris, and twelve man morris. Each game is similar in game play but restricts the number of pieces each person has. The game play itself is a simple two player three in a line game similar to Tic-Tac-Toe with slightly more complicated game play.

Nine Man Morris

Nine man morris is the most common morris variant. It is played on a board with 24 holes or spots to land on, as shown below.

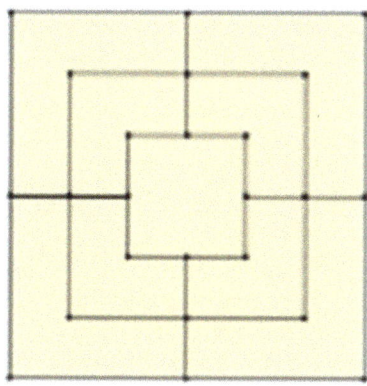

The game begins with each player receiving nine men, each player has different coloured men, often one player is white the other black, but this colour convention is by no means a rule. The object of the game is to get three of your men lined up along one of the lines, this is called a "Mill" and when a Mill is formed the player who formed the Mill is permitted to remove one of their opponent's men. The game is played in primarily two phases.

Phase 1:

Each player takes turns placing one man on the board at a time in one of the points or intersections on the board. If a Mill is formed during this phase the player is allowed to remove an opponent's man.

Phase 2:

Once all the pieces are on the board the second phase begins. Each player takes a turn moving one piece to an adjacent empty square with the goal of forming a mill. There is an optional rule called "flying" which enables a player reduced to only three men to move one man to any empty square instead of just an adjacent square. Flying strengthens the position of a weakened player allowing for possible come backs.

To win the game you must reduce your opponent down to two men or leave them with no legal move.

Three Man Morris

Three man morris, or "Nine Holes", is played on a grid similar to tic tac toe or in a board as shown below.

Each player in three man morris begins with three men each and is played much the same as nine man morris. Three man morris is won as soon as either player forms a mill, as such it is obviously a much faster paced game and is often over during the first phase of the game.

Six Man Morris

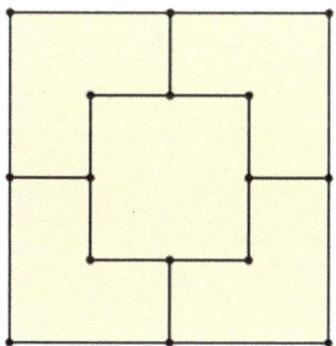

Six man morris, played the same as nine man morris, starts each player out with six men.

Twelve Man Morris

Played on the most complex of the standard morris boards, this version starts each player out with twelve men and allows for the additional creation of mills along the diagonal lines.

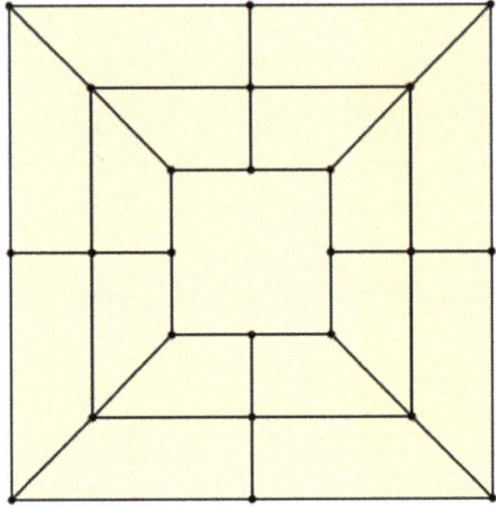

Alquerque

Alquerque or El qirkat is a game in a similar vein as tafl games, the board is similar and the pieces are similar. Like tafl games it is a capture based game. The board is initially set up as shown below. The game is played by players taking alternating turns moving one space at a time in any direction along a line. Players capture a piece by jumping over a piece to the next point (only if vacant) and taking the piece they jumped. (Wilkins, 2002)

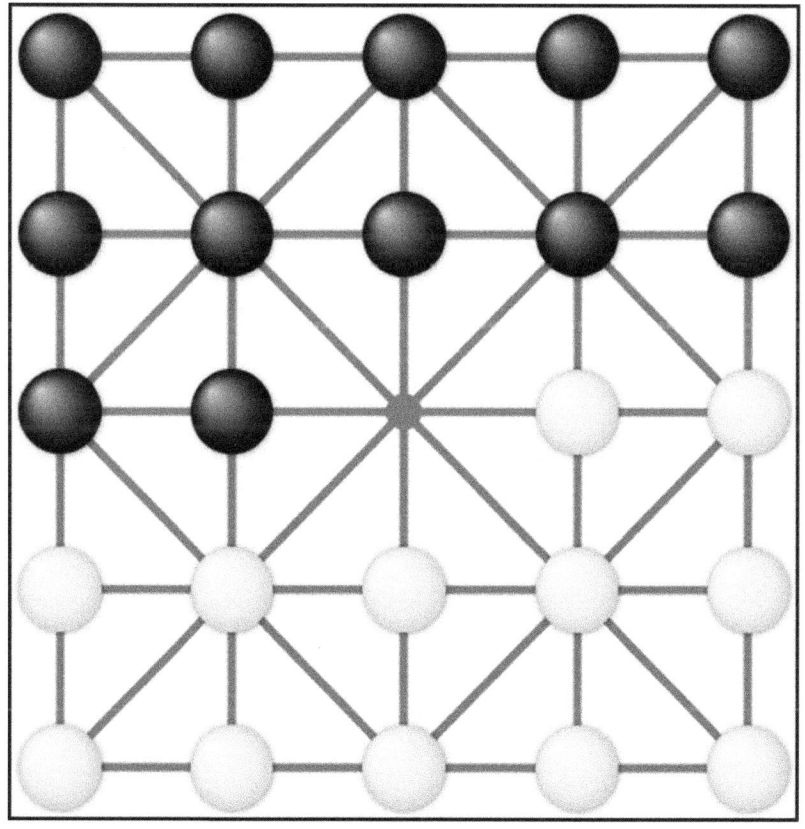

Alquerque initial setup

The game may seem quite simple, but the strategy involve in winning a game makes it quite a challenge. It's this aspect of the game that has made it a popular game throughout the ages. Its beginnings stretch back to the 2nd century in Egypt, but it became popular in Egypt through the Moors when they brought it to Spain during their invasion and subsequent occupation. (Bell, 1979)

Alquerque is considered a variant of Morris by many scholars, and while I believe it is in the same class of games I think by calling it a variant you ignore its complex history. Also considering how different the method of capturing pieces alquerque is from morris games I feel alquerque stands on its own. I believe the primary reason that game scholars place alquerque in the same family as morris games is because Alfonso X does so in his famous Book of Games. (Golladay, 2003)

Tables

Like tafl, tables is an entire family of board games all played using a modern backgammon game board, or a variation of said board. The exact historical origins of tables is lost, no one knows exactly. Like chess however, it is probable that it began in India or Persia and moved on from there. Similarity to the Indian game of Parcheesi cannot be ignored, thus many suppose that Parcheesi is an ancestor to tables (Jacoby & Crawford, 2000). Despite their clear differences myth holds that chess and tables are somehow linked, and that the family of games of tables would not exist without the game of chess. Muslim law even sees them as linked using them of examples of good and bad games. Chess is considered an intellectual game and therefore good, tables is seen as a game of chance and relies on destiny and is therefore bad. Both chess and tables games have been variety of restrictions around them. Muslim law suggest one should avoid games like chess, but that games like tables are outright banned. (Golladay, 2003)

H. J. R. Murray claimed, in his article "The Medieval Game of Backgammon" that there were over 25 different varieties of tables games played throughout Europe during the Middle Ages (Jacoby, et al., 1970). Alphonso X's book of games describes fifteen varieties of tables (Golladay, 2007). It seems likely the game spread rather quickly and each region developed their own variant, as well as new variants being developed using the same board as backgammon simply because it is cheaper to use an existing board than to devise an entirely new board. This dual use is the most logical explanation for games which share the board but do not resemble backgammon in any other way.

The word Backgammon did not become common use

for the family of games known as Tables until the 17th century. The word itself most likely is derived from Middle English for "back game" and became popular most likely due to the fact that most tables boards were two tables hinged together (Golladay, 2007).

Nard-Shir

Legend has it that the game of chess was invented in India and sent to the king of Persia as a Riddle. The Persian king's wise man solved the riddle of chess and created Nard-Shir and sent it back to the Indian King as a response (Golladay, 2003). Nardshir is simply the Arabic name for the entire family of games know known as tables or backgammon, but has now taken on the title of a particular variant of tables. Nard-shir takes its name from the pieces or men, nard means wood, and shir means lion (Golladay, 2007).

Nard-Shir, or simply Nard was extremely popular in Persia and spread throughout the Middle East. When the crusaders came, Nard became popular amongst the western soldiers occupying the land and eventually spread to Europe as the soldiers returned home. The game is very similar to modern backgammon with few differences the primary difference is there is no doubling bonuses or doubling cube.

When discussing Nard table the sections are usually described using letters starting at the top right hand corner and going around the board counter clockwise starting from A as shown above. There are a total of fifteen men for each player, usually one dark coloured and one light coloured.

							Dark Home Quadrant				
L	K	J	I	H	G		F	E	D	C	B	A

L	K	J	I	H	G	BAR	F	E	D	C	B	A
M	N	O	P	Q	R		S	T	U	V	W	X
							Light Home Quadrant				

Light player places three men in "Q", five is "S", two pieces in "A", and five in "L". Dark is a mirror image of light with three men in "H", five in "F", two in "X", and five in "M". In Nard, as in most Backgammon variants the men are laid out in a row. The object is to get all your men off the board before the other player does. To remove a man all your pieces must be in your home quadrant and you must roll exact number to take the piece off the board, for example if you have a piece on "V" and you are light then you must roll a three to get off the board.

The game is played with two dice, but the dice are not combined but seen as two separate turns. You may move the same piece twice to move the total of both dice, but it is seen as two moves, so both must be valid moves. A valid move is moving in a counter clockwise direction (light moves from "A" to "X", dark moves from "X" to "A") to a space that does not have two or more opponent pieces on it. A space with two or more pieces is considered safe and the men on that piece cannot be captured.

To capture a piece you must simply land on a space

that only has one opponent piece on it, this places them in the bar. A player re-enters from the bar on the home side of the opponent leaving from the bar. They cannot move from the bar unless the roll a number that they can safely move the piece from the bar to without landing on an opponent's safe space. A player with a piece on the bar cannot move any other piece until all pieces on the bar are back in play.

Some players deliberately keep a player in the bar by blocking as many of the spaces on the quadrant they must enter. This tactic is only advisable very early in the game.

Doublets

Doublets is a fast paced and simple tables game that is easy to learn and fun to play. Bell claims that the game was played in Iceland at the beginning of the twelfth century (Bell, 1979), and Francis Willughby included the game in his Book of Games from the 17th century, and it appears in Alphonso X's book of games as Doblet, although Alphonso's Doblet seems to be different than Willughby's descriptions and is quite possibly a completely different game. Murray calls Doblet a simpler form of Doublets, but Golladay disagrees with this sentiment (Golladay, 2007)

Doublets is played on only half of a standard backgammon board, two dice, and 30 men. Each player has 15 men each, for describing the layout and starting positions we will use the same notation as with Nard-Shir and the table is shown below.

Dark Home					
F	E	D	C	B	A
S	T	U	V	W	X
Light Home					

To set up Doublets white places two men are stacked in S, T, and U, and three in V, W, and X. The black men should be laid out in a mirror image to the white, so two men in F, E, and D, and three in C, B, and A. Notice that in doublets the men are stacked as opposed to laid out in a row.

The object of the game is to get all of your men off the board before your opponent. White rolls first, and both die are rolled at the same time, Cotton maintains that the players cast the die to find out who rolls first and that the player that rolls the highest on the die gets to roll first (Cotton, 1674). Each row equal a number moving from left to right between one and six, so if you roll a 2 and a 3 (and are white) you remove one man from T and one from U. The twist comes in when you roll doubles. You can remove on man for each point on the dice when doubles are rolled so if you roll two sixes you remove 12 men from your board. It doesn't matter which 12, you can choose which ones to remove. Obviously rolling doubles can seriously swing the balance of the game (Willughby, 2003).

Emperador

Emperador appears to be the same name for two different games, played much the same but with two different means of winning the game. One was popular in England, the other Spain (Jacoby, et al., 1970). It is claimed that Alphonso himself created this game, and since he fancied himself an Emperor rather than just a King and aspired to become the Holy Roman Emperor, the game was named Emperador or Emperor. (Golladay, 2007)

The game is played with a full tables board, three dice, and 15 men each. The initial setup is White begins with all 15 men placed on A, and Black begins with all 15 men placed on X. The goal of the game is to get all of your men off the board in your home quadrant before your opponent gets their men off of the board in their home quadrant, or to form a barata or prime. A barata is holding six consecutive spots with two or more pieces. If you manage to form a barata you win regardless of anything your opponent does. Barata's can only be formed on the second half of the board (or perhaps when at least one man has gotten to the second half of the board), the player forming the barata must also hit at least four of the opponents men, so while Barata seems like an easy win, it actually takes considerably more strategy then one would at first assume.

L	K	J	I	H	G		Dark Home Quadrant					
							F	E	D	C	B	A
						BAR						
M	N	O	P	Q	R		S	T	U	V	W	X
							Light Home Quadrant					

Like in most variant a single man is vulnerable to be taken and is sent to the bar. The re-enter from their starting quadrant and must make the trip around the table once again. Unlike all other variants there is a scenario in which a single piece on a space is not vulnerable, and this is on re-entry, when re-entering a piece may not take an already occupied space, even if that space is occupied by their own man. Should a player not be able to have his piece re-enter the game a tie is declared. (Golladay, 2007)

Medio Emperador

As the name implies, medio meaning half, Medio Emperador is a variant of Emperador played on half a tables board. It may be played with either two or three dice and it is up to the players to decide (Golladay, 2007).

Todas Tablas

Todas Tablas is a variant of tables that most resembles modern backgammon. It plays with two dice, and the opening arrangement is much like modern backgammon with white starting out with 5 in A, 2 in L, 5 in R, and 3 in T. Black mirrors this layout with 5 in X 2 in M, 5 in G, and 3 in E. If you have looked at the original manuscript for Alphonso's book of games you may notice that the starting positions are drawn different than I have described theme here. This discrepancy is to what is commonly believed to be an error by the artists. The description of the game in the book does not match the illuminations done by artists (Golladay, 2007).

						BAR	Dark Home Quadrant					
L	K	J	I	H	G		F	E	D	C	B	A
M	N	O	P	Q	R		S	T	U	V	W	X
							Light Home Quadrant					

Todas Tablas spread to England and by the 16th century it was commonly known as Irish. This is still a common variant to this day.

Reencontrat

Reencontrat is a tables game that is quite unlike modern backgammon. It is played on a full table, that is both halves are used, and players start with 15 men, but none are placed on the board. White begins at X, and black begins at L, both players move clockwise around the board. Before a man can play any other man the first man onto the board must make it completely around the board and off. Men can be captured and sent to the bar as in other variants, and recovering them is the same as well.

Game of The World

Game of the World, or Four Seasons Tables is a backgammon variant described in Alfonso book of games and is one of the most interesting variants in my opinion. It is played much like any other backgammon variant, but it is four player and is played on a round board. Traditionally there are four colours of men, each colour representing a season, thus earning the name Four Seasons Tables. The traditional colours are red for summer, black for autumn, white for winter, and green for spring. Normally the players are laid out around the table counter clockwise in the order of the seasons, red, then black, then white and finally green.

Each player starts on one of the four quadrants and with 12 men, none of the men are on the board to begin with. Three dice are rolled and the first player may begin placing his men on the board, no player can move off their starting quadrant until all players have all their men on the board. The order of turns played is clockwise around the board. Once all players have all of their men on the board they can begin moving their men clockwise around the board to their exit quadrant which will be diagonal to their own, or the third quadrant. To cast off their men they must get their men exactly on space beyond the last spot on their exit quadrant. Men that are cast off are taken off the board and are no longer in play.

Men are captured by an opponent land on an unguarded man. An unguarded man is a piece in a space by itself with no additional pieces to guard it. The captured piece is given back to the owner who cannot cast any men off until the captured piece is back in play by rolling it back onto his home quadrant (Golladay, 2007)

Detail from Alfonso X's book of games
four players playing The World

Chess

Chess is arguably the most popular board game ever to have existed. It has enjoyed enormous success throughout Eurasia, and even into parts of Africa. Unfortunately it is a game whose exact origins are lost to history, but most historians now agree that the game originated in India and quickly swept through Persia before finding popularity in Europe. There is almost no archaeological evidence of this early beginning of the game, but there is sufficient supportive evidence to suggest the theory of an Indian origin (Mark). The earliest estimates to the beginnings of chess date from 3000 BCE, but it could have begun as late as 570 CE. The strongest evidence for the Indian origin theory is that the pieces themselves represent the makeup of the forces of the Indian Army. While Elephants were known in the Middle East at the time, they were heavily used militarily in Europe. There is also the simple fact that in Indian chess all the pieces and phrases surrounding the game have a completely Indian origin, whereas in every other area there are trace elements of foreign influence in the naming conventions (Mark).

Finding the exact point and time in which Chess crossed over into the western world is nearly impossible, we can guess it is sometime before 1000 CE based on extant documentation. In the 1490's chess underwent its most massive rule change which brought the game quite close to its modern form, granting additional moves to pawns, vast power to bishops (and of course the change of the Elephant piece to the title of bishop), and most importantly the morphing of the fers into the queen and the granting of extreme power to the queen (Eales, 2007).

The game, then as now, was considered to be a way to hone strategy skills and thus improve military prowess. It is basically a simple war simulation each piece representing a class of soldier and each one's primary goal is to protect and serve the king. A more apt comparison to medieval life and warfare I cannot imagine.

The chess pieces and some rule changes have been made to chess over the years, but as stated the major changes occurred in the 1490s so it is certainly plausible to play chess in its modern variant as a medieval game.

Shartranj

Shartranj is more representative of the most common variant of chess played throughout the medieval times. These are older rules from Alfonso X of Spain, King of Castile, Leon, and Galicia. Alfonso sponsored the creation of a book of games called Libro de los Juegos that was completed in 1283. It's one of the earliest European book of games. In the book he lays out the rules for chess and a wide variety of variants.

The Pieces

- Shah/The King – Ruler of all, and lord of the army. As in modern chess the King of medieval chess can only move one space at a time, diagonally or straight, in any direction.

- Vizir/Fers – This is the equivalent of the queen, but the queen has not yet made the move to chess piece, although Alfonso does point out that some, who do not know better, refer to the fers as "Alfferza" which is a feminine form of Fers (Golladay, 2003). Fers is the king's advisor and carries the king's standard and his colours, this is probably the reason why in modern chess the queen starts on her colour. The fers in

medieval chess is a much weaker piece than the
modern queen, he can move only one square in
any direction at a time, but only diagonally,
never straight. On the first move the fers can
jump two squares, even if another piece is
blocking that path, however the fers cannot
capture if this jumping move is made, and the
leap is made only in forward directions and
cannot move sideways.

- Pil/Elephants – Modernly this becomes the
  bishops. The elephant can move two squares
  diagonally in any direction.

- Asp/Knights – In medieval chess as in modern
  chess it is common to refer to the knights as
  horses. The movement of the night in shatranj is
  the same as in modern chess, two squares in any
  direction, then one square at a right angle to its
  initial path.

- Rukh/Rooks/Chariot – While modernly
  represented as castles, Alfonso states that the
  rooks were made wide and stretched because
  they represent the ranking soldiers. Rooks can
  move straight as many unblocked spaces
  forward, back, right or left as they wish. Rooks
  were also sometimes represented as Chariots
  instead of castles or the ranking of soldiers.

- Piyadah/Pawns – The pawn has not undergone
  many changes over the years. The pawn can
  move only straight forward one square at a time,
  although an optional rule is to allow the first
  move to be two squares forward, this speeds up
  the number of moves before first contact with
  the enemy. However in shatranj the pawns may
  only move two squares on first move if no men

have been captured, once a man has been captured this ability is not available. The en passant rule had not yet been developed either.

The manner in which pieces are captured in this variant is pretty much the same as in modern chess. The pawns capture men one space on a forward diagonal only, and all others capture men on the space they can land on. Rooks however cannot capture a man on their first move. (Golladay, 2003)

Another variant layed out by Murray in History of Chess has the Fers named "Minister", and the Rook named "Chariot" (Golombek, 1976).

Four Seasons Chess

Acedrex de los quarto tiempos, or Four Seasons chess, was a four player variant of chess popular throughout Europe, but particularly in Spain. Each player would occupy a corner of the chess board, traditionally each player represented a season. Spring was green, summer red, autumn was black, and winter white. The moves were the same as in standard two player chess, but obviously with limited space on the board and limited men the game was faster paced. Alliances were not an official part of the game, but naturally were advantageous (Golombek, 1976). Each player had a King, Rook, Knight, Bishop, and four Pawns, there starting positions are shown in this image from Alfonso X's book of games.

Knight
King
Bishop
Rook

*Four Seasons Chess Starting positions from Alfonso X's
book of games*

On interesting feature of the Four Seasons chess is
when you checkmate one player you get to keep all the men
that player still has on the board and use them as your own.
When alliances are in play only the player who actually made
the checkmate gets the men of the fallen opponent. Keeping
fallen opponents men could grow your army to make you a
much more formidable opponent and can change the
dynamics of alliances drastically.

Byzantine Chess

Byzantine chess is a version played on a round board
and is more aptly called Round Chess by most chess

historians. There is a long standing belief that round chess was favoured by the Byzantines, however there is no clear evidence that this is so or that round chess was even known in the Byzantine Empire. It is played with the same pieces as standard chess or chaturaṅga and uses essentially the same rules. The main difference is that the board is round and players start on either end of the circle and go around the board in either direction to try to capture the king. (Murray, 1913)

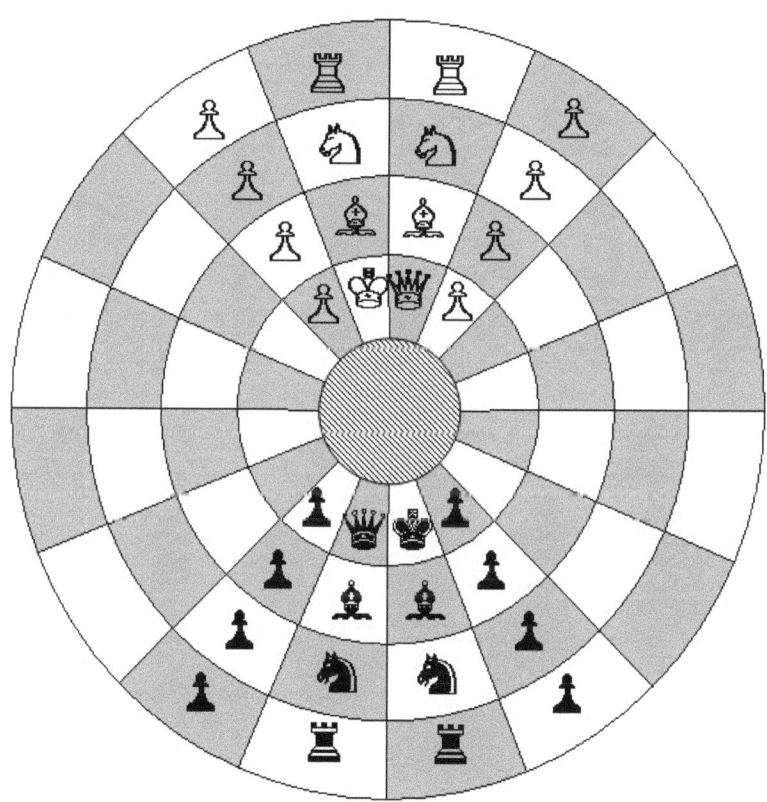

Starting Positions for Round Chess

In addition to the difference in the board there is another difference. Should two pawns from the same side heading in opposite directions meet each other, both pawns are illuminated by the opposition.

Citadel Chess

Like Byzantine Chess, citadel chess is played on a round board, the starting positions similar but reversed with the king and queen on the outer ring instead of the inner ring. The board in citadel chess has the center of the board divided into four, two of these are neutral, and the other two are the citadels. If a player gets his king into the citadel on the opposite side of the board a draw is forced. (Murray, 1913)

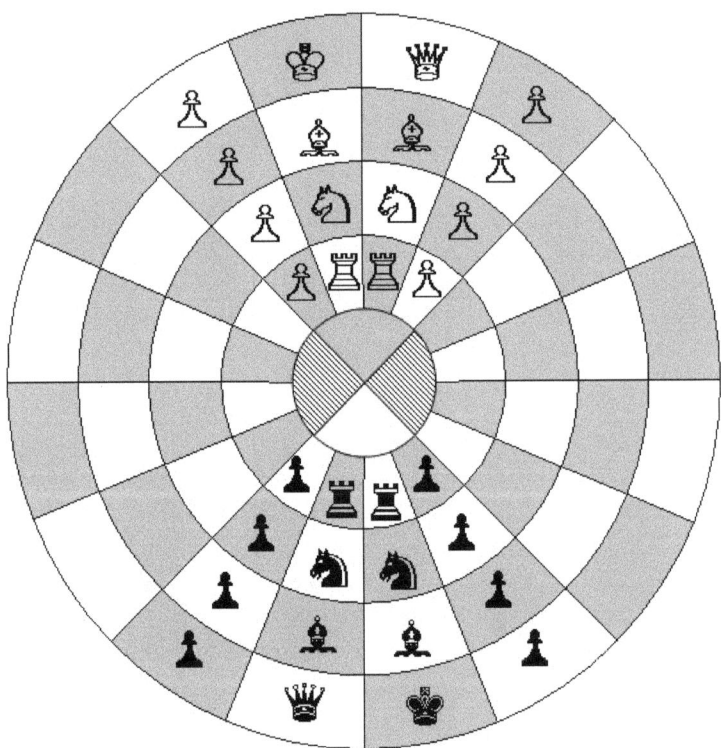

Starting positions of Citadel Chess

Games of Chance

"The urge to gamble is so universal and its practice so pleasurable, that I assume it must be evil."

Heywood Broun

It can certainly be argued that several of the board games mentioned above are games of chance. But since they all have elements of strategy as well, and the chance element is really just a feature of the game I thought a separate category for games which are played strictly with dice or other device of chance and little else made sense.

In each of these games the main component is some device of chance that is used to determine the outcome of the game. The most common device of chance is of course dice. However this is not the only device of chance used by medieval peoples. The teetotum was also a very popular and common device. The Dreidel, a common toy for Hanukkah toy, is a prime example of a four sided teetotum. Teetotums came in a variety of sizes with any number of sides and are great ways to play dice games without dice. Some claim that the teetotum really took off during the Victorian times in order to avoid clerical bans on dicing games, since a teetotum wasn't a die it could be used and still avoid any claim of breaking these rules.

12 sided Teetotum from Every boy's book: a complete encyclopædia of sports and amusements (Routledge, 1881)

Gambling was an extremely popular past time for medieval people. Pretty much every game in this book would have been gambled upon in one form or another, however some games lend themselves to gambling easier than others. Games of chance naturally are easier to gamble upon than any other. With chance taking the wheel it is hard to cheat, that being said loaded dice dating from the 15th century have been found and seem quite common. Often they would weigh the dice with drops of mercury ensuring the dice would always fall a certain way. The Museum of London has a cache of such dice in their collection, some numbered irregularly so as to always roll large numbers, others weighted as previously described.

In his 13th century book of games Alfonso X describes dice playing and dice making in considerable detail (University of Waterloo, 2010). Gambling was well known, and making dice was a serious trade.

Glückhaus

Glückhaus is a German dice gambling game using a board and two dice. Glückhaus translated to English means House of Fortune. The game was known in the 13th and 14th century as there are recorded sermons condemning it (Unknown, 2010).

To play every player puts a coin on the 7. Once all players have done so the first player rolls, if they roll any number except 2, 12, 4, or 7 they check that number on the board. If there are coins there they win the coins, if not they put a coin on that number. If a 7 is rolled the player puts a coin on 7. If a 2 is rolled the player gets to collect all the coins except the coins on 7, if no other coins are on the board the player puts a coin on 2. If a 12 is rolled the player takes all the coins. If a 4 is rolled the player does nothing. After the player rolls their turn they then pass the dice to the next player to the left and the game continues.

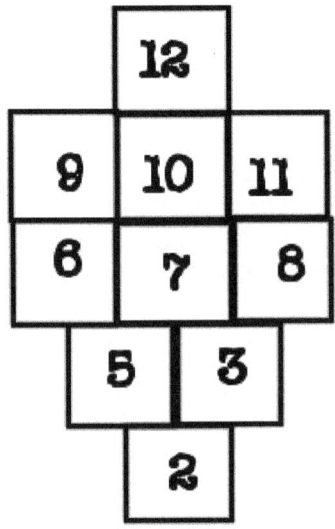

A simple Glückhaus board

Hazard

Hazard is game that appears complex at first. Once you begin to play it becomes simpler, and if one uses a game board it is extremely easy to follow. It is a gambling game that in many ways is similar to the modern casino game of craps. The game is rather fast paced, but during payout can slow down considerably. Historically fortunes have been won and lost at the hazard table. The game is mentioned in Chaucer's Canterbury Tales so it can be dated to at least as early as the 14th century without difficulty. (Chaucer, 1475)

The game is played with two dice, and players take turns as the host. The host rolls the dice. If he does not manage to roll between a 5 and a 9 then the players turn as host is done and the dice are passed to the left to the next player. If the player does roll between 5 and 9 then that number becomes their main, all other players place their bets, and the host must roll again for their chance number. Winnings are determined using the cart below, W's indicate a win and they win all the other players bets, an L indicates a loss and they must pay every player what that player bet, if there is no marking on the table then it goes into the playing phase.

CHANCE	MAIN				
	5	6	7	8	9
2	L	L	L	L	L
3	L	L	L	L	L
4					
5	W				
6		W			
7			W		
8				W	
9					W
10					
11	L	L	W	L	L
12	L	W	L	W	L

During play every player (except the host) can increase their bet between each roll of the dice. The host continues to roll the dice until he rolls either his main (first roll) or his chance (second roll). If he rolls his main, he wins all the money bet by the other players and remains as host for another round. If rolls his chance however he loses and must pay each player whatever they bet and passes the dice on to the next player on the left who becomes the new host.

A variant can be played in which if the main roll is not between 5 and 9 the player has to continually roll until they do get a number between 5 and 9.

Triga

Triga is a simple gambling game, and it requires three dice and at least two players. Essentially everyone puts in their stake, and whoever rolls a Triga first wins. A triga is a three of a kind or a roll equalling the high scores of 15, 16, 17, or 18, or alternately the low scores of 6, 5, or 4. The first player who rolls these numbers wins the pot (Golladay, 2007). No source I found recommends the order the players play, so I suggest the following method to make the system fair, while still making it an interesting gambling game. A player does not put a coin in until it is their turn to roll the dice, if they roll a Triga they win the pot, if not their coin remains in the pot and the next player puts a coin in the pot and rolls continuing around with every player putting in a new coin to gain another roll. Should a player quit before the pot is won their stake is forfeit to the pot and it remains for whoever can roll a triga next. This system allows for new players to join or leave at any time, and allows for the pot to continue to grow.

Put and Take

Put and Take is a medieval game that uses a four sided teetotum. The game is really quite simple. First, everyone puts a coin in the pot then you take a four sided teetotum with the number's one through four on them and give the teetotum a spin. If the number one turns up you put a coin in the pot. If a number two turns up you do nothing, if a number three turns up you put a coin in the pot. Finally if a number four turns up you win the pot.

There is no limit to how many people can play at a time, play rotates around the players clockwise.

Those familiar with the Jewish Hanukah tradition of spinning a dreidel will recognize this game, as this is exactly how that game is played as well, but with Hebrew letters instead of numbers (University of Waterloo, 2010).

In another variant a six sided teetotum, or dice is used, scoring changes to:

1. Take one from the pot

2. Everyone puts one coin in the pot

3. Take all from the pot

4. Put two in the pot

5. Take two from the pot

6. Put one in the pot

Shut the Box

Shut the box is definitely a late medieval development, its history is surprisingly difficult to trace given its relatively late beginnings. It appears to have originated in Northern France, possibly Normandy (Masters, Shut the Box - History and Useful Information, 1997). Some say that it originated in the 18th century, which would put it out of range for the medieval times, however there is some evidence that it goes back even further and possibly as early as the 15th century. The game was a popular pastime for sailors on ships as it was easy to transport.

Shut the box By Roland Scheicher / Roland Scheicher at German Wikipedia (Own work (Original text: "eigenes Foto")) [Public domain], via Wikimedia Commons

To start the game all the numbers are turned up, the object is to be able to turn down all the numbers, and thus "Shut the Box". To do so the player takes a pair of dice and rolls, whatever the total between the two dice is the same as the total of the numbers they must turn down, so if they roll a 5 they can turn down 1 and 4, 2 and 3, or 5. Player continues until they no longer have a valid move. Their score would be the total of all the remaining tiles, the player with the lowest number of tiles wins. Some variants had tiles going up to 12 as well. As with many dice games wagers were often placed on the playing of shut the box, both by players and by spectators, but gambling isn't an integral part of the game and playing for sport was just as common as playing for money.

Le Drinquet

Le Drinquet is a French dice game documented throughout medieval literature. Period rules to the game do not seem to exist, however a description by Frans Semrau was written in his 1910 scholarly work on dice games in literature entitled Wurfel und Wufelspiel im alten Frankreicht. The game is a fairly straight forward game played on a chess board. It is not, by default, a gambling game, but can easily be converted to one.

The game is played with two players, a chess board, and anywhere from 1-3 dice depending on the players' preference. Each player is assigned either white squares or black squares on the chess board. The players take turns throwing the dice onto the chess board. In order for a point to be counted the dice must land completely in one of the player's squares. If the white player rolls three dice any dice counted must be on a white square with no part of the dice touching the edge or in a black square. First player to score more than a hundred points wins. It is probably advisable to have a tally sheet handy for scorekeeping. (Knutson, 2010)

Card Games

"The cards always look different when it's your turn to play them; loaded with subtly different possibilities."

Alastair Reynolds

Medieval man has had a love/hate relationship with cards, sometimes banning them as evil or sinful forms of gambling, and sometimes enjoying them as the fun way to pass time.

Cards have evolved over the years, the familiar modern form with four suits being hearts, spades, clubs, and diamonds was not the norm; this was known as the French Deck. A much more common medieval deck was the Mameluke Deck whose suits were batons, coins, swords, and cups.

Cards were often a means of sending a political message, as they were borderline sinful and having a deck of cards with questionable images was just adding a little fuel to the fire.

The 16th century Flötner deck, sometimes referred to as the "poop deck" is just such a satirical deck. The Flötner deck contains humours images of monks getting drunk, farting, vomiting, and yes sometimes defecating. The deck reportedly was designed in 1545 by a German artist Peter Flötner who is known for his scatological humour in art (Flötner).

The deck varied in other ways other than suits. The Jack card for instance was sometimes called the Knave card, sometimes the Knight card, and sometimes wasn't included at all. They were sometimes not even rectangular, the deck famously called the Cloisters Deck, or the Flemish Hunting Deck currently residing in the Cloisters Collection of the Metropolitan Museum of Art are a wonderful example of oval shaped cards.

General Card Rules

In most medieval card games there is terminology for playing order that does not seem to vary much from game to game. It is a reasonable assumption that this order was followed even in games that did not specify this order. The youngest player is the initial dealer, the eldest sits next to him and plays first. This does not strictly relate to age, but rather general terms used for card playing. When a hand or trick is won however the player that won the trick then proceeds to go first for the next round and is now considered the eldest. In all cases of ties the eldest of the players with the winning hand wins.

In some games there is a trump suite. A card of the trump suit automatically outranks any card of any other suit. The cards in the trump suit follow the normal valuations for that game.

In trick taking games a trick is one round around the table each player playing one card. In these games there is often, but not always a trump suite. The winner of the trick is the player who has the highest valued card in that round and collects the cards played in that trick and piles them in front of him for easy scoring at the end of the hand.

Noddy

Noddy is a card game that bears a striking resemblance to Cribbage, and any fan of Crib would love this faster paced version. Simply put noddy is crib without the crib. There are references to Noddy dating back as far as 1550 but it was Randle Holms in 1688 who provided us with a brief glimpse of how it was played.

> 2 or 4 may play at it, 61 being up. Each perfon hath 3 cards and one turned up to which he makes as many casts as he can. They are thus merkett, Flat back or King of Spads is six, Countenance or Queen of Hearts, four, Knave of the trump, 2, Knave of Hearts 5, a pair 4, pair Riall 12, a pair Taunt 24. Every 15 as you can make is 2, and every 25 is 2. In playing down the cards you have the same advantage of 15, 25, paires &c. and the next to 31 hath 1 cast, if he make 31, there is 2 casts. (Holme, 1688)

Dealing the Cards

Noddy uses a traditional 52 card deck. The game is generally played with two players, although three or four could play, in the case of four partners could be played. Each player is dealt three cards. After dealing, the top card, in what remains of the deck, is turned up. This is the "Noddy Card", if said card is a Jack then it is said to be the "Knave Noddy". Aces in Noddy are always counted as 1 never 11 and order is always A234...JQK ace never follows a King. All face cards (ace not included) are worth 10 points.

Scoring Points

- *Knave Noddy* 1pt if in the hand 2pts to the player who did not deal if it is turned up

- *15, 25, or 31* - 1pt per card that made up the fifteen, i.e. if a 3 a 2 and a 10 are used to make fifteen then the total points is 3

- *Pairs* - 2pts

- *Pair Royal* - aka three of a kind 6pts

- *Double Pair Royal* - aka four of a kind 12pts

- *Runs up to Five Cards* - 2pts if a run of three, any runs greater than three is 1pt per card

- *Flush* - Three or more cards of the same suit 1pt per constituent card.

Announcing Points

Before the hand is played, the player who did not deal announces, but does not show, the points in his hand. After this announcement the dealer announces his points. Each player pegs their score.

Playing the Hand You Were Dealt

The player who did not deal starts, plays any card in their hand, announces its value, and then turns alternate. Any time a player creates a scoring combination from the cards played thus far they can peg the points. The running total for played cards cannot be greater than 31, if any player cannot play a card without going over this number they must pass. Any cards left unplayed at the end are irrelevant, there is no second round.

Winning

Noddy is generally played to 31 pegged points, score can be kept on a scorecard, counters such as poker chips, or a peg board such as you would see in crib.

Cribbage

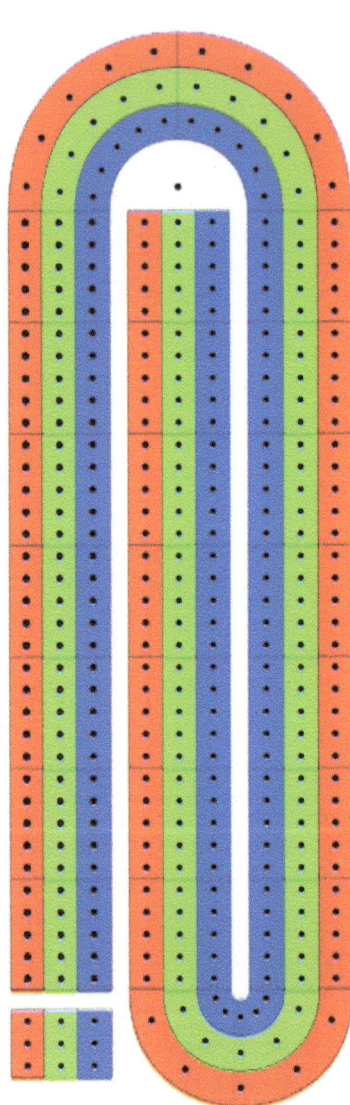

Standard Cribbage Board (Gunther, 2013)

Cribbage is still one of the most common card games played today, but it has a rich history. To call it a medieval card game is playing a little fast and loose with the definition of medieval, but I think it is close enough. The earliest references to cribbage state that the noted poet Sir John Suckling invented the game in the early 17th century based on the game Noddy. There is no truly reputable source for stating this is absolute fact though what is more likely is that he codified the rules of a Noddy variant that were already fairly popular (Masters, 1997). I believe it logical to assume that the game had been developing for at least fifty to a hundred years prior to being codified by Sir John Suckling.

The specific variant of Cribbage codified by Suckling was what is now called Five Card Cribbage as opposed to the game most commonly played now which is six card cribbage. As you can probably guess the main difference between five and six card cribbage is the number of cards dealt per hand.

The game is usually played using a peg board for scoring, although keeping track of the score using other methods should not be an issue. A standard medieval crib board has two rows of 60 holes and an extra hole at the end for the winning point, using a modern crib board is acceptable, but makes for a slightly longer game.

As with almost all medieval card games the Ace in cribbage is only ever worth one point, as it is really the one card and not a face card. Number cards (2-10) are worth their face value, and face cards (J, Q, and K) are worth ten.

Dealing the Cards

Medieval Cribbage seems to be primarily a two player game. Using a standard 52 card deck both players are dealt five cards each. Players alternate at being the dealer, as always the youngest player deals first.

Start Card

The player who did not deal should cut the remaining deck after the cards have been dealt and turn over the card there, this will be the start card. If this card is a Jack the dealer automatically can peg 2 points.

Discard

Each player must discard two cards from their hand into the crib. The points in the crib will count towards the dealers points so discarded cards should be considered carefully, much of the strategy in Crib comes from knowing which cards to keep and which to throw. At times you may break up points in your hand in order to keep the dealer from gaining points, while at others you may want to give the dealer points in order to maximize your own scoring potential. If you are the dealer the strategy of the discard isn't quite as important as regardless you are getting any points discarded.

Game Play

The player who did not deal starts off the game play discarding one card from his hand and adding it to the value of the start card and announcing the value. The turns alternate until either player cannot play a card and stay at or under 31, the player that cannot play a card under 31 "Go", if the other player can still play and stay at or under 31 the player can play those cards. Once both players cannot play and stay at or under 31 then gameplay stops, the last player who was able to play scores a point or 2 points if the value was exactly 31.

Scoring during gameplay is no different than scoring during modern cribbage gameplay. 2 points for fifteen, 2 points for a pair, 6 for Pair Royal (three of a kind), 12 points for Double Pair Royal (four of a kind), one point for each card in a run.

In the case of a run the cards do not have to be played in order, so if 7-9-6 were played the player who played the 6 would score three.

Announcing Points

An astute reader will note that announcing points comes after gameplay in Cribbage vs. before gameplay in Noddy. It is my belief, completely impossible to prove, that the reason the points announcement was moved to after gameplay was to reduce instances of cheating. To catch someone cheating at Noddy you had to really pay attention to what was played vs. the points announced, in cribbage you can, and indeed must, show the cards as you announce them. More than any other detail this is the primary difference between Noddy and Cribbage, in Noddy cheating was almost expected, whereas in Cribbage attempts have clearly been made to reduce cheating.

Point scoring is pretty much the same in announcing as in game play, but with the addition of the flush, one point for each card of the same suit if there are three or more of the same suit (start card can be used in adding up your points).

Also if you have a Jack of the same suit as the start card you get "One for His Nob".

The non-dealing player counts first, then the dealer. The dealer counts his natural hand first, then the crib (the discarded cards from the discard stage).

Wining

When one player pegs more than 61 that player wins. It is not necessary to hit 61 exactly, if you get more points than 61 you still win.

One and Thirty

The game of thirty one is still a common game played, I know I played it as a child quite often. The Oxford Dictionary of Card Games claims that this game has been around since at least the fifteenth century (Parlett, 1996). The simplicity of the game lends credence to the fact that the game has probably been around for a very long time.

One and Thirty is played with two or more players using a traditional 52 card deck. Three cards are dealt to each player. Once the cards are dealt each player is asked if they will stick or if they want another card, if they want another card the dealer draws one from **the bottom of the deck** for them. Once all players have stuck then the players lay down their cards in order they were dealt. If a player is over 31 points then they are out. The player closest to 31 points without going over wins the game.

Gambling Variant

As with almost any medieval game, gambling was a big part of One and Thirty. Played much like blackjack when gambling is involved however there was no doubling down just simply bet at the beginning, Willughby seems to imply that the dealer was not actually playing. When gambling a player that hits 31 exactly is hitter and wins double (Willughby, 2003). Why anyone would play as a dealer when they are simply paying out is beyond me, I would have to assume that the dealer was playing, but as a banker and against all players and winning all bets if the dealer hits exactly 31 before any player does.

Bon Ace

Bon Ace is a One and Thirty variant in which you deal the last card of the three cards dealt to each player face up. This is the players' first scoring opportunity. The player with the highest turned up card wins a counter from all other players, this indicates the game would be played as a betting game or with counters such as poker chips.

This is also one of the rare circumstances in medieval card games in which the ace is a high card. In Bon Ace an Ace beats all other cards during the face card counting, but is still only worth one during gameplay, the Ace of Hearts is the "Bon Ace" and beats all (Willughby, 2003).

The rest of the game is played the same as a normal game of One and Thirty.

Hannikin Canst Abide It

Hannikin Canst Abide it is a One and Thirty Variant in which you only count up to fifteen instead of thirty one, you are also only dealt one card at a time. The dealer than asks each player "Hannikin Cans't Abide it" to which the player says "he can" if he wants another card, or "he cannot" if he does not want another card. (Willughby, 2003).

Laugh and Lie Down

Laugh and Lie down is a simple card game reminiscent of the popular children's card game of Go-Fish, but much more complex. References to the game can be found dating back as far as the 16th century (Parlett, Laugh and Lie Down, 2013). This game is clearly primarily a betting game as it is stated in the rules that the each player stakes two and the dealer stakes three.

Dealing the Cards

Five players are dealt eight cards each. The remaining cards are placed face up so every card is visible but in no pattern. Once dealt anyone with a four of a kind must play them immediately to their pile of played cards. If the table cards contain a four of a kind these go to the dealer. If the dealer misses a four of a kind and play begins the four of a kind is fair game for anyone who spots it and this does not count as their turn.

Game Play

At each turn the player must lay down a pair from either their hand or from their hand and a card laying face up on the table (not from the cards played by others). If during their turn a player cannot lay down a pair then that player must lay his cards down with the cards on the table. All the other players then laugh at him (thus the name laugh and lie down).

The pairs you play go in one pile as your won cards. Four of a kinds and three of a kinds found afterwards are to be played as pairs only.

Game play continues until only one player has cards left. This player automatically wins 5 counters (whatever you are using as betting chips), all untaken table cards get added to the dealers won cards.

Pay Off

All players count the number of won cards they have. Any player who did not manage to win eight cards must pay 1 counter into the pot for every two cards short of eight. For example: If you have five cards won you would owe 2 counters into the pot. Any player with over eight cards takes 1 counter for every two cards over eight that they won. (Willughby, 2003)

Ruffe & Trump

Ruffe and Trump is a simple partnered trick taking game. Two teams of two are required to play this game. Team members sit alternating as in Euchre and most team trick taking games. The game uses a standard 52 card deck, all the cards are used. Often Ruffe and Trump was played as a betting game for a shilling per set (52 points).

This is one of the rare medieval card games where the Ace is valued at 11 points instead of just 1. The Ace is the most powerful card of any suit, and the Ace of the trump suit beats all.

Dealing the Cards

Youngest player deals first, and as usual eldest player plays first. Each player is dealt 12 cards apiece, but instead of alternating around the table each player is dealt four cards at a time before moving to the next player. After the cards are dealt there will be four cards the top card of the left overs (which is called "the head") is turned upright. The upturned card on the head determines the trump suit. All cards of this suit automatically beat any other card of any other suit.

Ruff

The ruff is basically your strongest suit. Announcing the ruff is a stage of the game right after dealing in which you announce the number of cards in your ruff, the player with the most cards in their ruff gets 12 points for their team, however they have to show their ruff to confirm that they do indeed have as many cards as they claim. While the 12 points is an advantage in the game having to show your cards could be a decided disadvantage. Since there seems to be no method for verifying that you aren't underbidding your ruff it is plausible to assume you could do this to avoid having to show your cards. If the trump suit is your ruff you can count the turned up head card as part of your ruff.

Rubbing the Head

Once the ruff is won the player with the ace of trump may rub the head, or take the head as their own cards, if the ace of trump is turned up, or in the head, the dealer gets to rub the head.

Game Play

Game is played as a normal trick taking game. The value of each card is pretty standard, number cards from two to ten are their face value, face cards are worth ten, and the ace is worth eleven.

In any basic trick taking game a trick is one round around the table each player playing one card. The winner of the trick is the player who played the highest valued card of the same suit, or the highest value trump card, all off suit non trump cards played have no value.

The eldest leads for the first trick, and the winner of the trick leads thereafter. Players must follow suit, play continues until for twelve rounds or all the players, except the player who rubbed the head who should at this point have four cards remaining which get included in that players points. Points are then accounted for. Count the number of cards each team won, any over 24 cards get counted. So if one team has 40 cards in their won pile they would get 16 points.

The game finishes when one team or the other reaches 52 points. (Willughby, 2003)

Single Hand Ruffe and Trump

Single hand Ruffe and Trump is a variant in which each

player plays for themselves and not as on a team. The game play and scoring is the same, with the exception of points being accounted start at 12 cards instead of 24, so any player having over 12 cards scores the number of cards over 12. (Willughby, 2003)

Three player Ruffe and Trump

Three player ruffe and trump is exactly what it sounds like. Basically the same game as single hand ruffe and trump, but with three players instead of four. The only difference really is that it instead of taking the entire head when you rub the head you only take the top four cards. (Willughby, 2003)

Trump

Trump is a ruffe and trump variant that is played exactly the same, but with no ruff. (Willughby, 2003)

Gleeke

Gleek is a three player trick taking game with a poker like start. While the rules sound complex and seem difficult, once play begins it becomes fairly easy to follow.

Stakes

Gleek is a gambling game and as such counters of some sort must be used. Ffor the purposes of these rules we will refer to the counter as chips.

Value of the Cards

In most medieval card games Ace is counted as a one, however Gleek is the exception to this rule, in Gleek the order of cards is A,K,Q,J,10,9,8,7,6,5,4. Threes and twos are removed from the deck prior to dealing. Each card has specific point values listed below;

Ace (called the Tib in Gleek)	15
Jack (Knave)	9
King	3
Queen	3

Ante

Each player must put 1 chip into the pot before the deal begins.

Deal

Each player is dealt 12 cards in three batches of four cards, the remaining eight cards are placed in the middle as the stock and the top card from this pile is turned up for trump. If the turned up card is a four this is called Tiddy and the dealer automatically gets four chips from each player. As in most medieval card games seating arrangements starts at the eldest, then progresses to the left to the youngest, the youngest deals first and the eldest gets first bid at the stock and goes first. Deal then passes to the left as normal.

Gameplay

Each hand has four parts;

1. Bidding the stock
2. Vying the Ruff
3. Claiming mournivals and gleeks
4. Trick Play

Bidding the Stock

After the deal, each player may look at their cards and decide if they want to bid on the stock to try to improve their hand. The first player to bid (eldest in the first hand) must bid 12 chips, the others may pass or bid more according to how much they want to change their hand. Bidding continues until all other players pass. The player with the highest bid must discard 7 cards and take the entire stock except the turned up trump card. The amount that player bid then gets divided between the two other players, if there is an uneven number of chips bid then the extra chip goes in the pot.

Vying the Ruff

Vying the ruff is a stage in which the players bet on who has the highest scoring cards in any one suit. To count up the value of your ruff, you add 10 points for any court card (King, Queen, Jack), 11 points for the ace, and face cards are worth their face value. Four of a kind (called a mournival) of Aces automatically wins the ruff, but it is the only mournival that can be counted, all others must be of the same suit. When the betting starts if all players pass and no one bets the vying phase is skipped over and the pot remains and is doubled for the next round. Once one player bids, the next player may either see, see and raise, or pass. Passing is the same as folding, seeing matches the most recent bet, and seeing and raising is matching the bet and upping it by a certain amount. Betting continues until either two players pass causing the remaining player to win the bet, or until all players have either passed or seen and raised. If there are two or more players who have seen and are thus still in the vying stage they must show their ruff, the player with the highest scoring ruff wins the pot.

Claiming Mournivals and Gleeks

A mounival, as discussed above is a four of a kind, a gleek is a three of a kind. Each player declares their largest gleek or Mournival and the player with the highest set wins this round and each player must pay the requisite number of chips to the winner. A gleek of jacks is 1 chip, of queens 2, of kings 3 and of aces 4, mounivals double these values. Gleeks and mounivals of face cards are not counted (alternate every player gets paid for every gleek or mounival in their hand)

Trick Play

At any time during trick play if the four of trump (the Tiddy) is played each player must pay 2 chips to the player who played the Tiddy. Beyond that trick play is played pretty much like any trick taking game. The first player lays down a card, each player must then lay down their highest card in that suit if they have a card in that suit, if they do not then they may play a trump card or any other card. The highest card in suit, or the highest trump takes the trick, and that player leads the next trick. When you play an honour (Ace, King, Queen, Jack) you must announce that fact.

After all cards are played add 3 points for each trick

you took and add up the points for the cards you took according to the point value chart above. If the turn up card was an Ace, King, Queen, or Jack then the dealer counts that point. Any player who did not get 22 points total must put one chip in the pot for every point below 22, any player who scored above 22 gets one chip for every point above 22, any player who scored exactly 22 neither gets nor pays any chips. (Willughby, 2003)

Beast

According to Francis Willughby Beast or Le Beste was invented in France and migrated to England to become a very popular game in gambling houses. Its exact true origins have been lost so it is impossible to determine how old the game is. A clue to it being a later period game is that the Ace is a high card, since all early card games had the Ace as simply worth one point it can be assumed that Beast was invented later on when it became a little more common to use the Ace as more than just a value of one. The game is played with four players, although both a five and six player variant is recorded in Willughby's book of games. It is a trick taking gambling game with fairly complex rules, but can be quite a fast paced game.

To play Beast you use a standard 52 card deck and remove the 2 through 6, although Willughby does maintain that leaving the cards in the deck does not seriously alter the game, so playing with a full deck is feasible (Willughby, 2003).

Each player must stake two coins into the pot except the dealer who stakes three. The dealer extra coin the dealer stakes placed in front of them to signify they are the dealer, at the end of the hand the dealer's extra stake gets added to the pot and the new dealer must stake an extra coin in front of them to signify they are the new dealer.

The dealer deals three cards to each player (three at a time instead of what modern card players are used to, being one at a time), and then two more to each player for a total of five cards each.

The dealer then places the deck in the middle of the table and turns up the top card, and this card's suit becomes trump. As in other trump based games, the trump beats all other cards.

Once all the cards are dealt and the trump has been determined each player examines their cards to see if they believe they can win at least two tricks. The player to the right of the dealer gets first option if they feel they can win two tricks they say "I play", if they feel they cannot they say "I pass". The first player to say "I play" becomes the player. If one player has said "I play" it goes around a second time and the players will now say "I counter" if they believe they can beat the player. If everyone passes the next player to be dealer stakes an additional coin to the pot (none others add to the pot) and collects all the cards to deal the next hand, otherwise the hand continues. Any player that has passed does not continue playing the hand, as a general rule it is good advice to counter if any player declares they will play, the risk is none and there is always the chance you will beat the player.

The player starts the hand and plays a card, the other players must follow suit, if they are caught not following suit they are said to have Renounced, and if you are caught renouncing you must put the same number of coins that is currently in the pot into the pot yourself. If a player does not have the suit but they do have trump they must play the trump or they are also renouncing.

If a player has the Ace, King and Queen of trump (or basically the top three trump cards still in play if one of these three cards is the turned up trump card), that player many win by demonstration, that is throw down the three cards and the hand is done. If you have the top three trump you don't need to demonstrate, it is just a way you can speed up play. If you want to drag out the torture on your fellow players, feel free, it can add to the fun.

Winning two tricks is not a guarantee of winning the hand, any other player could win three tricks and "Beast" the player, you can also Beast the player by winning the first two tricks, if you are a player who has countered and you win the first two tricks you have won by Beast and win the pot. The player must win three tricks to guarantee his win, or win two and no other player gets the rest of the tricks, if he manages that he wins the hand and the pot (Willughby, 2003).

Five and Six Player Variants

The game can be played with five or six players instead of four. With five players six cards are dealt to each player three cards at a time, and the sixes are left in the deck. With six player Beast the sixes and sevens are left in the deck and seven cards are dealt to each player first four then three. Theoretically you can do any number of players as long as you still have cards to add to the deck, always deal one more card to each player then there are total players (Willughby, 2003).

Losing Lodum

Losing Lodum (or Loadum, Load Him) is a kind of reverse trick taking game, the object is to take as few tricks with scoring cards, or loader cards, as possible. The game can be traced back to the late 1500's, but there is no documentation for this game being played any earlier than that. Francis Willughby's Book of Games is one of the only extant descriptions of how the game was played.

Willughby does describe the game as a gambling game, however there appears to be no advantage to the gambling aspect of the game and as such it need not be played as one, to play as a gambling game each player puts in their stake, and the last player remaining wins the pot. There is no limit to the number of players in losing lodum, and the entire deck is dealt out. This will mean that some players may end up with more cards than others, but that is simply part of the game.

Each player is given three counters, stones, coins, or any such thing can be used as counters. Some cards, called loader cards, have specific values, and a player when a player gets loader cards equalling 31 points they are lose that hand and have to surrender a counter. Once a player has no more counters, they are out of the game. The last player with any counters wins.

Loader Card Values	
Ace	11
Ten	10
Jack	1
Queen	2
King	3

The dealer deals one card at a time, and deals the entire deck. There is a trump in this trick taking game, but trump is not determined until play begins. The eldest player leads the first trick by playing any card they wish, each player then plays one card, suit must be followed if possible. If it is not possible to follow suit the player plays any other card, this suit becomes trump at this point. The highest trump card, or if no trump was played, the highest card of the lead suit in a trick wins the trick. If a player does not follow suit when they could have, and they get caught, that player loses all their remaining counters and are out of the game. The winner of each trick leads the next trick.

When the trump card is declared (the first time a player cannot follow suit) that card is set aside but turned face down. The trump card is only shown the one at this time, it is announced then turned down. Each player is then responsible for remembering the trump card. If trump is played, but another player forgets this is a trump card and claims the trick as their own no other players need remind them of this fact, and the player who claimed the trick keeps it. This is called swallowing the trick.

If you suspect a player has 31 points worth of loaders in their taken tricks you may challenge them. If you issue a challenge the player must show his loader cards taken, if they equal 31 he is out and the hand ends. You may challenge if you take a trick that brings your loader points to 31, but if you think another player already had 31 points. If the player you challenge has 31 points they lose a counter, but you do not. If they did not have 31 points you lose a counter and they don't. Regardless of how it is determined, once a player reaches 31 loader points the hand is over and the eldest player becomes the dealer and a new hand is dealt. Obviously the challenge rule implies that admitting you have 31 points is not necessary, and you can simply bluff your way through.

If you have an unguarded loader in your hand you may request an exchange at any point during the hand. A guarded loader is a loader in your hand in which you have several low value cards of the same suit, for example if you have the ten of spades but you also have the two, three, and five of spades the ten is guarded. To make an exchange you simply ask if anyone will trade, if it is Jack, Queen or King you specifically ask to trade a "card for a card", for the Ace or Ten you request to trade a "coat for a coat". If someone agrees to the trade you exchange cards, if they are the same suit the cards are returned to the original owners, if they are different suits the exchange occurs. All exchanges are final if they are different, but if no one agrees to make an exchange then you have no choice but to keep the unguarded loader.

If all cards are played and no one has reached 31 points all players show their loaders and the player with the most points in loaders loses a counter. Naturally it is possible, in this case, for a player to have more than 31 points and still not lose, if another player has an even higher score that player loses their counter (Willughby, 2003).

Winning Lodum

Winning Lodum is a variant of Losing Lodum, played much the same, but essentially in reverse. Each player starts out with no counters, and the first player to reach 3 counters wins. In winning lodum the idea is to get to 31 points as quickly as possible, doing so ends the hand and gains you a counter (Willughby, 2003). There is not as much subterfuge or strategy involved in winning lodum compared to losing lodum.

Whehee

This is the card game that is just as fun to say as to play. Whehee is a quick game that can be used to pass time quickly, and pretty much anyone of any age can learn this game in no time. A standard 52 deck of cards is used, each player is dealt three cards. The player whose hand is all one suit is the whehee and thus the winner, if there is more than one whehee then the eldest wins. If no one is whehee then swap cards, eldest hands a card to the next player and that player must give the eldest one of their cards and so it goes from player to player until someone finally becomes whehee and wins. (Willughby, 2003)

Karnoffel

Karnoffel, or Kaiserspiel as it is sometimes called, is often identified as the earliest known European card game. Dating back as early as 1426 in Germany. Variations on the game are still played in Switzerland. Karnoffel is a simple partner based trick-taking game with trump suits played with four players (two teams of two) (Parlett, 1992).

A sermon delivered in 1521 gives some great details on the game pointing out that Karnoffel is "topsy-turvy" to other card games at the time. It points out that in Karnoffel lower valued cards can end up more powerful than the suited cards, thus a King can be taken out by a Jack and even the numbered cards have the capability to take suited cards. The sermon goes on to point out that in every hand a different card can become the most powerful card in the deck all by the luck of the draw (Voss, 1930).

Karnoffel is played with a deck of 48 German suited cards, which is a standard deck with the aces removed. In German suit there is no Queen or Jack, just the King the Ober and the Unter. If you are playing with a French suit deck the Queen can be used as the Ober and the Jack as the Unter. The seating arrangement is the players alternate and partners sit across from each other with opponents on either side as shown in the table below.

Team 1	Team 2
Team 2	Team 1

The dealer deals one card face up to each player. The lowest ranking face up card determines the trump suit, in cases of ties the first of the dealt cards becomes trump. The dealer deals four more cards to each player face down, cards are dealt one at a time as in most card games. Once all cards are dealt the players pick up the cards and the play begins. The player to the left of the dealer leads the first trick, the winner of each trick leads then next trick. The team that wins the most tricks wins the hand.

Winning a trick is fairly complex, in most cases it is simply the highest valued card of the suit that was led, but when it comes to the trump suit there are some very special cards that have considerable power, it is these cards that are referred to in the sermon mentioned earlier.

Trump Cards and how they are played:

- Karnoffel: Unter of Trump beats all cards.

- Devil: 7 of trump, beats all cards except the Karnoffel, but only when led, and the devil cannot be led on the first trick of the hand.

- Pope: 6 of trump, beats all cards except the above.

- Kaiser: 2 of trump, beats all cards except the above.

- Oberstecher: 3 of trump, beats all cards except the King of the suit led or any of the above trump cards.

- Unterstecher: 4 of trump, beats all cards except the King, or the Ober of the suit led, or any of the above trump cards.

- Farbenstecher: 5 of trump, beats all cards except the King, Ober, or Unter of the suit led, or any of the above trump cards.

No other trump cards carry any weight except as the face value of the cards (Fontananera, 1993).

Landsknecht

As the name suggests, landsknecht is a game of Germanic origins, most likely in and around the 16th century. The earliest written mention of this game is from *Gargantua* by Rabelais originally published in 1534. It lists the game as lansquenet. *Gargantua* is a great starting resource for medieval games, because at one point in the book Rabelais just straight out lists every game the main character is good at, and it is extensive (Rabelais, 1894). The game was popular throughout the 16th century but fell out of favor by the 18th despite die hard German fans managing to get it declared as Germany's national card game. It was revived in the 19th century for a brief time, but never really managed to regain its former popularity.

The game is a very simple gambling game in which the dealer, called the banker, has a distinct advantage. There is no real strategy involved in the play, it is purely a luck of the draw game. The game was very popular with German mercenaries who wanted to just gamble their loot, but not think overly much.

The role of banker can be determined one of two ways. In friendly games the role would pass from player to player around the table, or a player could declare himself banker and challenge all comers. There is no real limit to the number of players, but the banker must have enough coin to cover the bets of all players, this is the only real risk to being the banker. The banker is staking much more per game then the individual players, but the payoff is more for the banker as well.

Each hand is an individual game, so players can change out often, much like modern blackjack in casinos. The play begins as soon as each player, but not the banker, antes up.

The banker starts out dealing two "Hand Cards" in the centre of the table then one card for himself and a "Rejouissance" card for the players (only one card, not a card each). If any of the first four cards dealt can make a pair then the hand is done and the dealer wins all bets. If no pair is made in the first four cards play continues. Once the rejouissance is dealt the players place their bets on that card and may increase their bet if they wish.

The banker then draws one card and places it in the middle of the table near the Hand Cards. If the card matches either of the hand cards it is placed beside the hand card and the banker draws the next card. If the card matches any of the player's rejouissance cards the dealer wins the bets on that card and the player must ante up again on that card. If the card matches the banker's card the banker must pay each player whatever they bet and the game ends. If the card matches a rejouissance card the dealer wins all bets on that card and that card is removed as a rejouissance and placed on the bottom of the deck. If no cards are matched then this card becomes an additional rejouissance and players may bet on this card as well. The game ends when all cards are played or there are no remaining rejouissance cards (Nelson, 2007).

Simplified Multiplayer Variant

This variant is technically more complex, but it does simplify the betting process, and thus makes it an easier game to actually play with multiple players. Each player plays against the bank individually, instead of all players playing against the bank as a group.

In this variant there is no rejouissance card, but rather each player get their own card which acts as their personal rejouissance card. In this variant the player's individual card may match another player's card, but it still must not match the dealer's card nor the Hand Cards or that player loses their bet and is out of the game for that round. The banker then plays one card at a time to an individual player around the table. While this slightly weakens the banker's advantage it also lessens his risk, so it could be considered to balance out in the end.

Primero

Primero is an early form of poker, that is not to say that poker is a direct descendant of primero, but that the games are similar, while there is no linear progression from primero to poker the similarities between the games cannot be ignored. Primero is a vying game with a number of speciality hands and bluffing is a prime component.

The earliest reference to Primero seems to be Gerolamo Cardano's *Libre de Ludo Aleae* or The Book on Games of Chance dated 1520. Shakespeare makes repeated reference to the game in numerous plays, so it can be presumed that it was a very popular game during his lifetime.

The card values in primero are fairly unique. It takes a little getting used to, but after a few hands it becomes second nature, it could be a good idea to have a table of card values handy for scoring purposes. The game is played with a standard 52 card deck with the 8, 9, and 10's removed.

Card	Value
Ace	*16 Points*
2	*12 Points*
3	*13 Points*
4	*14 Points*
5	*15 Points* .
6	*18 Points*
7	*21 Points*
Court Cards	*10 Points*

Like poker there are specialty hands, there are a total of five possible hands in primero, from lowest ranking hand to highest the hands are:

- Numerus: Two or three cards in a given suit, this hand is only worth the point value of the two cards in that suit.

- Primero: One card from each suit, each card can be counted in a primero, so the hand is worth the point value of all the cards added up.

- Supremus: 6, 7, and Ace of a given suit. A Supremus is always worth 55 points.

- Fluxus: This is a flush, four cards of the same suit. The value of the hand is the value of each card added up.

- Chorus: This is a Primero, but specifically four cards of the same face, not just the same value, but the same cards, so four 2's or four Kings, etc.. The point value of this hand is the value of each card added up.

The dealer deals two cards to each player face down. Once the cards are dealt each player can look at their cards. Once the players have looked at the cards the betting stage begins. The eldest player has the option to vie, place an initial bet, or he can fold or pass each player gets their chance around the table from eldest to youngest until all have seen.

When a player sees the bet they are matching what has been vied and continuing on.

If a player passes, they may discard one or two cards from their hand and draw the same number from the deck. If a player folds they may take back half the money they have bet and leave the remainder in the pot but they are out of the game for that hand.

When a player vies they declare the best hand they believe they can make, and they must actually make at least the hand they declared in order to win. They must declare both a hand and a value to continue. If there is already a bet on the table then they must beat the value of the cards in the current hand type or bid a higher ranking hand type, so if the bid is "Numerus 25" a player must bid either a higher valued Numerus hand or bid Primero or higher hand. You may discard one or both cards if you vie, but that will most likely give away that you are purely hoping to pull off the hand you are bidding and that you have no real idea if you can. A player may bet whatever amount they wish when vying. If a player cannot match what has been bet they can go all in and if they win they only win from each player the amount they bid, the rest of the pot goes to the second highest hand.

The last player in a vying round must see if the other two players pass. So if you have player 1, 2, 3 and 4, player 1 passes, player 2 vies, player 3 passes, and player 4 passes. It then gets back to player 1 and player 1 must see regardless of his hand, player 2 then passes, but does not discard since he has already vied, and players 3 and 4 have to either see or fold. If no one vies in the first round of the first two cards dealt it is a dead hand and the eldest player now becomes the new dealer. If at least one player vied, and all other players have seen or folded then it goes on to the next phase where two more cards are dealt and the betting process begins all over again.

Bluffing is a huge part of the strategy of Primero, however there are some rules around what sort of bluffing is allowed when it comes to bidding on your hand. You may see on a vie of primero if you have a supremus, or if you have a chorus you can claim either a primero or fluxus. Other than that you may not bluff about what hand type you have, you may however bluff about the hand value, you can underestimate your hand value to draw in more bets, but you cannot underestimate your hand type.

Once all players have had a chance to see then the players who have not folded show their cards. The player with the highest valued hand that is at least the value vied in the hand type declared wins the pot. Unless as previously mentioned they ran out of money and had to go all in, then they win the amount they bet from each player, the rest of the pot goes to the next highest hand, if there is no next highest hand then the remaining bets remain in the pot for the next hand. In cases of ties the eldest hand wins. You must show all of your cards to demonstrate that the hand you declared and that you don't have a better hand that would have won.

It is possible for no one to win, this occurs when the player who vied bluffed and failed to get a hand valued at least what they vied and no other player got a hand of at least as high as was vied. If no one wins the money remains in the pot until the next round to be won then.

It is probably best for each player to keep the amount they are betting in front of them directly so the amount bet can easily be tracked for cases of folding, or going all in. When there is no winner the remaining bets on the table can be pushed into a central pot.

English Primero

English Primero should be considered a separate variant from the more common Italian version of the game as sources often describe the game with a few notable differences. The English variety is played much the same, it is only in vying that differs. In English primero if a player runs out of money he is out of the hand, whereas in Italian Primero the player can continue to vie for the part of the pot that he can cover. The Italian version allows a player who has folded to take back half of the bets he put into the pot. The English variant does not allow this, any money you bet remains in the pot until won.

There is also no bidding in the English variety, and this can dramatically alter the game. Essentially this means that the best hand wins and there is no bidding specific hands, so when you are betting you are betting you have the best hand not that you have the best Fluxus (for example). The English version is a little faster, but there is less emphasis on out bluffing your opponents (Coeur, 2003) (Suzuki, 1994).

Piquet

Piquet, or Cent (or Saunt) as it was known as in England, is a two player trick taking game that is quite easy to learn despite its apparent complexity. It was a well-known game by the end of the 15th century and is heavily covered in various documents. Rabelais mentions the game in his novel Gargantua and Pantagruel (Rabelais, 1894).

Piquet is one of the rare medieval card games where the Ace is considered a high card. The two through six of each suit is removed leaving a deck of 32 cards in play. The game can be played with a deck of 36 as well by leaving the sixes in, Cotton (who wrote *The Complete Gamester* in 1674) seems partial this method over the 32 card deck. Both are acceptable, there is no advantage or disadvantage to either method (Coeur, 1995). The rank of the cards in ascending order is 7, 8, 9, 10, J, Q, K, A. The value of the cards is pretty standard, with court cards being worth ten, pip cards worth their stated value, and aces worth eleven.

The Deal

The dealer deals twelve cards to each player four cards at a time. The remaining cards are called the Talon or the Stock and are placed between the players. Once the hand is dealt the hand is into a variety of steps, Blanks, Draw, Ruff, Sequence, Sets, Tricks, and Pique and Repeque. Scores are counted at each phase. If you forget to count, or miscount your scores during any of the scoring phases you cannot correct this, the count you declare is the count you have to go with. If a player catches you lying about your count in any phase that player scores all your points for that phase.

Blanks and Draws

Blanks and Draw are generally considered one step, it

starts by the elder declaring if they have a blank, and a blank is a hand with no court cards and no aces. If the elder declares a blank, but the younger does not have a blank the elder is awarded ten points and the players move on to the draw. The elder may discard up to eight cards, but must discard at least one and draws new cards to replace the cards they discarded from the Talon. The younger may now discard and draw up to eight, but at least one card from the Talon.

Counting Ruffs

Next is the counting of Ruffs. A ruff is the number of points in a given suit. The elder declares how many points they have in their largest ruff, if the younger has a ruff of equal or higher points they then declare their points. If the ruffs are equal no points are awarded, if not then the player with the higher ruff may take the points in their ruff as follows; 1 point is awarded for each ten points in the ruff, rounding is allowed so if your ruff was worth 55 you would score 6 points, however if it was 54 you would only score 5. The loser may demand to see the winning ruff, doing so is strategically wise as it may grant the loser an advantage in the trick taking phase of the hand.

Sequences

Once points are recorded for the Ruff the players move on to counting sequences. A sequence is three or more cards in sequence such as 10, J, Q. The eldest player declares his longest sequence and the high card in that sequence, if the youngest has a longer sequence or a sequence of the same length but with a higher high card they declare it. If both players have the same length sequence and the same high card no points are awarded, however if one of the players has a higher high card or a longer sequence that player is awarded points as follows; for sequences of three 3 points is awarded; for sequences of four 4 points are awarded; any sequence over 5 ten points plus the number of cards in the sequence is awarded. Once again the loser can demand to see the winning sequence.

Sets

Sets are counted next, sets are three or more of any card valued at ten or higher. The elder declares his highest set of highest cards, if the younger has a set of greater number or equal number but greater card value (if the elder has three Jacks, the younger can declare if he has a set of three Queens or higher, or four 10's). The player with the highest set is awarded points. A set of three is worth thirteen points and a set of four is worth fourteen. The loser may demand to see the winning set.

Tricks

Tricks are played like any standard trick taking game without trump. First the elder leads, then the younger must follow suit if they can, if they can't the elder takes that trick, if they can and beat the elder's card the younger takes the trick. The winner of each trick leads the next trick. Points are awarded during trick play and at the end of the hand. Every trick in which at least one of the cards was ten or over earns the winner of that trick 1 point for each card over ten. Winner of the final trick scores an additional 1 point (on top of any points awarded for cards ten or over). After all tricks are played the player with the most tricks takes ten points (if both players take six tricks no points are awarded). If a player managed to win all the tricks he scores a Capet which is worth 40 points instead of 10.

Pique and Repique

If a player manages to get 30 points before the other player scores anything that player gets a bonus 30 points, this is called Pique. If the player manages to get a Pique before the trick taking phase this is called a Repique and is worth an additional 30 points for a total bonus score of 60.

Winning the Game

Piquet is generally played to 100 points. It is common to keep track of points on paper, although a crib board can be used for scoring as well. If you alter the points needed to win it throws the balance of the game off considerably, as in the standard game a Repique is pretty much a guaranteed win when the game only goes to 100 points (Miller).

Team Sports

"The glory of sport is born at the moment when the game and the person become one, when all the complexity of one's life finds a moment to emerge in the game. "
Timothy Shriver, Ph.D.

Team sports have always been popular, they are all about showing the superiority of your group over others. Militaries have always promoted team sports to promote team building, it was no different in the medieval world then it is now.

Team sports are more likely to be a game for the masses than games for nobility, nobility was more inclined to prove individual superiority, whereas the lower classes are more likely to promote regional superiority. Often games would take place between neighbouring towns or villages, and often a friendly rivalry would develop. Many games gathered large groups of spectators. Shrovetide football games were known to garner huge crowds to watch the games.

While many team sports needed large fields to play in, they didn't usually need to be dedicated areas, they could be common areas, farmed fields, or pretty much anywhere. Curling, as an example, began being played on frozen rivers, Stoolball began in churchyards. This is in stark contrast to the more "civilized" individual sports like tennis that required large areas be dedicated to the sport, and thus required wealth and status.

Curling

Its forty-two pounds of polished granite, bevelled on the belly and a handle a human being can hold. And it may have no practical purpose in itself but it is a repository of human possibility and if its handled just right, it will exact the kind of poetry Chris Cutter (Paul Gross) describing a curling rock *(Gross, 2002)*

(Stirling Stone)

Scottish tradition holds that the game was invented in Scotland. I see no reason to question this belief, however it should be noted that the game spread quickly throughout Europe. Pieter Bruegel the Elder, the Dutch artist known well to anyone who has researched medieval games, painted two pictures showing curlers in the background, these are *Zyklus der Montsbilder*, and *Winterland mit Vogelfalle* both painted in 1565.

The oldest record of Curling comes in the form of a curling rock with an inscription, the inscription reads "St Js B Stirling 1511". The stone doesn't resemble modern curling stones as most people might recognize them, it is a style known as a "loofie". A loofie is just a smooth rock with a handle jut directly into the rock itself. The word Loofie is a derivative of the Scottish word for hand. Loofies would soon be replaced with smooth river rocks with handles attached to them and thus the modern curling rock begins to take shape (Lodi Curling Club, 2007).

Curling is simple by concept, complex in execution. It is more a strategy game than anything. A curling sheet (playing area) is set up with a target area called house, in the centre of the target area is the button. The idea is get your rock closes to the button of the target area house, all rocks that are closer to the button than the closest opponent rock count. Each team takes turn throwing the rocks down the ice until each team has thrown eight rocks. The specific medieval rules and layout of a sheet are hard to determine, in all probability they haven't changed drastically and it is reasonable to assume that the modern rules with very little variation would work for recreating a medieval curling match.

Winterlandschaft mit Vogelfalle (Winterscape with a bird) 1565

Zyklus der Monatsbilder (The Hunters in the Snow) 1565

Stoolball

es vaches garcer ne porra mes entenore

(Ghistelles Hours)

Stoolball is a simple bat and ball game along the same lines as Baseball, Cricket, Rounders, and other similar games. Stoolball, sometimes known as Sto-Ball, Stowball, Stumpball, and Stob Ball appears to be the father of both baseball and cricket predating both game. The sad truth about stoolball is that the original rules to the game have long been lost to history, while there is considerable documentation to the game being played there is no record of how it was played. Luckily it is a popular sport in modern day Sussex UK, while the rules are not likely to quite match up with the medieval version, and there is a considerable gap in time between the medieval game being played and the modern version where no records of the game being played exist, it is possible extrapolate plausible rules from these modern versions and what we do know about how the game was played in the medieval times.

For some unknown reason modern stoolball has replaced the traditional stools with wickets similar to cricket. This might have been to entice cricket players to accept the game when trying to reintroduce the game to players (Stoolball England). We do know however that traditionally the game was played with milking stools, although sometimes tree stumps would act as the stools, or essentially anything else that could act as a "base".

As with many medieval sports the first literary mention of stoolball comes in the form of a warning from the church. In 1450 John Myrc recorded a warning by a 14th Century Vicar that said "Bats and bares and suche play/Out of chyrche-yorde put away" (Henderson, 1947) in the manuscript by Myrc there was a written in addition of a specific list of banned sports, "tenessyng handball, fott ball stoil ball and all manner other games out churchyard" (Block, 2006). Stoil Ball is a clear reference to stoolball.

Balls that would be used during the medieval times were generally leather balls stuffed with various fillings from grass clippings to cloth to feathers. Wood shavings was a common filler, but probably too hard to use for modern recreation. I have found that a leather ball stuffed as tight as possible with scrap cloth works very well.

Stoolball, while played at other times of the year, was viewed as an Easter celebratory sport. Often the winning team would be presented with a tansy cake, although how the association of tansy cakes and stoolball formed is completely unknown. Stoolball was also one of the few co-ed sports. Both men and women played the game and usually intermingled. For this it was often seen as a great way to meet prospective mates. (Henderson, 1947)

I have taken some creative license in recreating the rules of medieval stoolball. I borrowed from others who have blazed the trail in recreating the rules of this medieval game, specifically Wendi Dunlap who has spent considerable time researching and testing the rules. My main assumption in developing the rules is that medieval sports often had as few rules as possible they were generally decided upon on the spot, especially in the case of peasant games such as stoolball. I believe these rules are fairly plausible to how the game would have been played in the medieval ages but have no way to verify these rules so anyone recreating a medieval game of stoolball should naturally feel free to adapt the rules according to their tastes if they find these rules lacking in any way.

To play the game you need two teams, the size of the teams is fairly irrelevant. You could in theory play one on one stoolball, but I would recommend team sizes of at least three players. The teams should have the same number of players though to ensure balance. Like baseball and cricket one team starts out at bat and one team starts out fielding.

Equipment

Stoolball equipment built for Wendi Dunlap to recreate a game of stoolball, image copyright by Wendi Dunlap, all rights reserved, used with permission.

- At least one bat, bat styles vary from anything from a large pingpong paddle to a standard cricket bat, to a baseball bat.

- At least two stools, or objects to act as stool.

- At least one ball.

Object

The object of the game is to score as many runs as possible. To do this the team at bat must hit the ball thrown by the fielding teams bowler, when they do so they can run from the batting line to the base stool(s) and then back to the home stool, the batter can then run back around the base stool(s) and back to home if they have not been called out (how to call out a batter will be covered in its own section below). The fielding team's objective is to get the batter out before they score runs. Fielders do NOT use baseball gloves. By tradition stoolball is a co-ed game, women and men play together.

Teams

Each team should have at least three players present or they forfeit the game. A maximum of 10 players per team is recommended as much more than this tends to be too chaotic.

Each team must have at least three players each. Each team will only play as many players as the lowest number team, for example if one team has three players and the other has ten then both teams will only play three players per inning. The teams can agree upon a lower number of players so they can have alternates on the bench.

Positions

Stoolball has three basic position, the fielding team consists of several fielders and a bowler, equivalent to the pitchers position in baseball. The opposing team has only one batter on the field at a time. Additionally the fielding team my choose to have a back catcher, but this is not a required positon and the fielders can really stand wherever they think the best chance of catching the ball will be. There is no need for basemen at all.

Innings

Like modern baseball stoolball has innings. An inning lasts for an entire rotation through the roster. Each player gets a turn at bat during an inning. If there are alternates available on a team it would be acceptable to have some who only field and some who only bat, otherwise every player must take their turn at bat.

Bowling

The Bowler must stand in line with the base stool between the base stool and the field stool. The bowler must throw underhanded. All throws must at least make it to the batter line without touching the ground to be a valid bowl. The bowler's objective is to hit the home stool without the ball hitting the ground first, if he does so the batter is out and the next batter approaches the batter's line, or if all batters have been at bat the inning is over.

Batter is out

To get a batter out the fielding team must get the ball and throw the ball at the home stool from the field side of the batters line. If they do so the batter is out.

Batter

Batter must stand on the batting line. There are no balls, fowls, or strikes. The batter can take as many swings as they need to as long as the ball hasn't hit the home stool. Any contact of the bat with the ball is a valid hit, once the ball his hit the batter must run from the batter's line around the base stool(s) counterclockwise. During game play I have found that if the fielding team does not have a back catcher often a good strategy is to attempt to hit the ball behind you, this can be accomplished quite easily with practice with a bat style closer to cricket than with a baseball bat.

Field Layout

This can be agreed by the players, and there are no hard and fast rules on this. There is evidence of multiple base stools as well as just one. There can be any number of stools, but there can only be one home stool, and must at least be one base stool. Stoolball can be played with one, two, three, or more base stools according to whim.

Something must be used to mark the batters line. It can be some rope, scrap cloth, or anything that won't trip the runners but still clearly mark the line. The batters line should be 6 feet from the home stool. The rest of the stools can be laid out according to how the players agree, but it is recommend that one stool be set 30 feet from the batters line in a straight line between the home stool and the batters line (so a total of at least 36 feet is required).

Common Optional Rules

- Soak 'em Rule: the fielding team may tag out the batter by hitting the batter with the ball, throwing it or tagging them. The fielder must be on the base stool side of the batters line.

- Retaliation Rule: when the team at bat takes the field, if the bowler picks up the ball before the fielding team has cleared the field the previous fielding team loses their turn at bat.

- Brave Batter Rule: batter must hit the ball with his bare hands instead of a bat

- Stop Running Rule: Batters can stop at base stools similar to baseball

- Other rules can be invented on site, as long as the players agree to them.

Hurley

The history of Hurley is quite important in Irish history. Early Irish legends claim that often Hurley was used to settle disputes between towns, and there are even examples where a game of Hurley was used to avert war. How true these tales are is hard to say, but it is certainly an important part of Irish culture. One of the earliest written references of Hurley comes from *The Book of Leinster* written sometime in the 12th century by an unknown author. It recounts the tale of *Táin Bó Cúalnge*, or *The Youthful Deeds of Cú Chulainn* set in the 1st century AD. Cú Chulainn is one of Ireland's most celebrated legendary historical figures. In the Táin Bó Cúalnge it claims that Cú Chulainn's prized childhood possessions that he took everywhere with him were his javelin, and his silver Sliotar (hurley ball) and his bronze hurleystick (O'Rahilly, 1967).

Hurley, or Hurling as it is modernly called, is an Irish game akin to field hockey. It is played with Hurley sticks (shown on the right), which are similar to field hockey sticks but have a flat round end instead of a curved end and a slight lip to catch

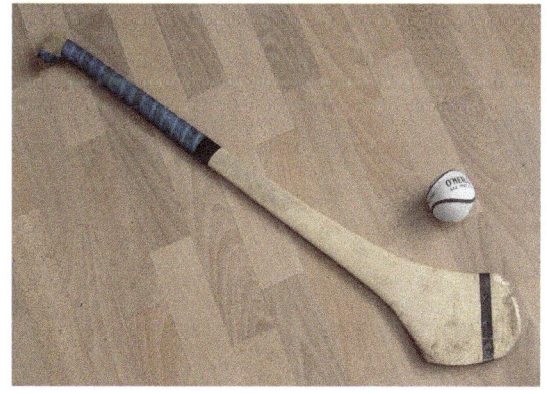

Hurley and Ball by Dr. Peter Wöllauer

the ball. The ball, in modern Hurley is a leather bound cork ball similar to a baseball, however in Medieval Ireland the ball was usually boxwood or metal, often silver or bronze. The ball in Hurley is called a sliotar.

The game is played with two teams, the size of the team is not specified, and there are records of teams in the thousands taking the field all at once. Each player has a hurley made of wood or bronze, and this hurley's primary use is for carrying the sliotar, but it could also be used as a weapon to check other players, or outright bludgeon them (though in modern play this is a). The ball can be touched in hurley, but not if it is on the ground, and it can't be carried more than a few paces (modern rules state four but medieval rules are unclear). In general the ball is carried down the field either balanced on the end of the hurley (thus the lip) or hit with the hurley to another player.

In modern hurley the goal posts are shaped like an H. The posts are 6.4 meters apart and stand 4.88 meters tall with the cross bar at the midway point. A shot over the crossbar is one point, and under is three, however there is nothing in the historical texts which indicate this is the case, and simply appears that there were simple goal posts and if the sliotar made it through the goal posts it was a point. Unlike football and other such games the players are not divided on the centre line, players from both teams can be on either side of the centre line. One or two players, called Mid-fielders, from each team line up on the centre line, and the referee throws the sliotar in the air between the mid-fielders to start the game.

If the ball goes out of bounds the team that knocked the ball out of bounds loses control and the other team may, using their hurley, and not touching the sliotar with their hands, hit the ball back into play. If a goal is scored or an attempt to score has missed the goaltender may throw the ball back into play (in modern rules from within the goal crease), all other players must be at least 20 meters back.

There is no indication that in medieval hurley there were specific positions, but modernly there certainly are. Shown are the positions for one side, naturally the other team would have mirroring positions.

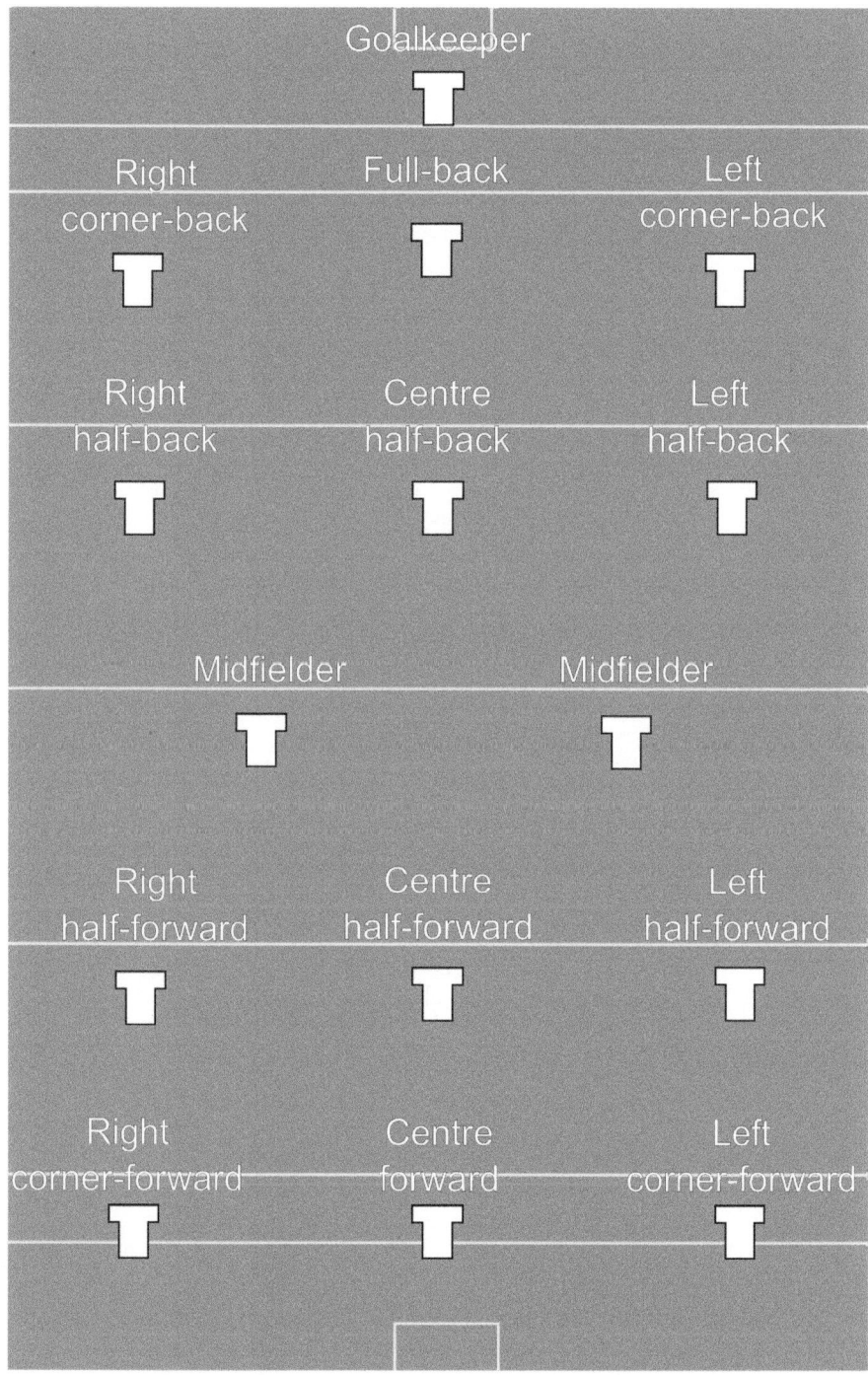

Knattleikr

Knattleikr is a Viking sport that appears throughout the Norse sagas as a popular game played by all ages and nobility and commoners alike (Thordarson). It was a pretty violent and rough full contact sport. Hurstwic, a Massachusetts based Viking Recreation group has done considerable work to redact workable rules. Unlike many Viking sports Knattleikr did not seem to be brought over when the Vikings made their way throughout Europe and the sport died out leaving nothing but references in the Sagas about the game.

Beyond Hurstwic, others have tried to redact reasonable rules for Knattleikr based on the little evidence we have, although it cannot be said with any certainty that any of the rules fit with how it was played. We know the sport was played with bat and ball, and that there were goal posts. It seems the players were divided into two teams though there seems to be no limit to the size of the teams. We know that the sport was full contact, primarily due to the fact that the Sagas report several injuries to the players. Beyond these few facts we know next to nothing about the game.

Due to how much work I know they put into it, I tend to believe that Hurstwic probably has the most accurate rule set for the game of any others I have come across.

Equipment

- Each player has a bat, a 4' long 1" diameter dowel seems to make a good one, however the Sagas do state that it was possible to trap the ball with the bat, so probably something more like a cricket bat would work better.

- A field is required and two areas to be used as the goal

- One ball, a felted wool ball, or leather ball would be accurate. The Sagas suggest a hard ball, and a wood ball would work for this, but I would suggest a softer ball.

Game Play

One team starts out with the ball. The two teams face off against each other, a player from the team with the ball pitches it towards a player on the opposite team. If that player hits the ball the ball is then in play. If not, then the team that had the ball loses it and the other team now pitches. Once the ball is in play it remains in play until someone scores. If the ball goes out of bounds then the player who last had the ball before it went out of bounds or who currently had it loses control and the ball is handed to a player on the other team. Once the ball passes into the goal a point is scored.

Players may use any means necessary short of killing another player, to get the ball from a player. Common methods include tripping, tackling, grappling and grabbing the other player. The bats may be used to trip other players, but may not be used to bludgeon another player (there is no evidence that bludgeoning another player was not allowed during Viking play, but this rule is usually added for safety sake).

Winning the Game

The team that scored the most goals at the end of the game wins. The game ends when there is no more beer to drink, or there is only one player left standing (Hurstwic LLC, 2006). There is no real time limit on how long the game might last, several Saga sources claim games would often go on for days.

Football

When most of the world thinks about football they think of kicking a ball around a field towards one of two nets and kicking it in the net for points, and no touching the ball with the hands. In other words what North American's call Soccer. When North American's think of football they think of a game that is mainly played by running a ball down a field towards goal line with the ball in hand. Surprisingly from a medieval standpoint both games could and should keep the name football, both were played within the period generally referred to as the Medieval Times. And in point of fact, what most of the world calls "American Football" is more akin to the game as it was played than what America calls "Soccer".

Commonly it is argued that Soccer should always be called football because it is played with your feet, and that American football is a bastardization of the game that should use the name handball or some similar suggestion. This logic states that the very name football was used because the sport was played with the feet, but in actuality the name derives from a whole class of games that are played on foot rather than horseback or some other form. So the name football is derived because it is a ball game played on foot, and not a ball game played with the feet.

The word Soccer is actually an abbreviation with some good old 19th century slang idioms thrown in for good measure. Soccer refers specifically to Association Rules Football. Association was shortened to Soc, and an "er" was added to the end because it was a common practice in England in the early 19th century to add an "er" on the end of words, so Rugby became Rugger, and the word Soccer was invented (Ekblom, 1994).

Games like football have existed as far back as ancient Greece, who called the game "episkyros". The Romans called it "harpastum". Not surprisingly the first written reference we have of the game called football comes from an edict banning it, specifically one from John Myrc in 1450 stating "tenessyng handball, **fott ball** stoil ball and all manner other games out churchyard" (Block, 2006).

In Britain the game reached nearly fanatical status, it was not a game for nobles, but rather a rough and tumble game played by commoners. Injuries and property damage was common when a game broke out. Shrove Tuesday was a particularly common date to play football on, in fact it was so common the game even became known as Shrovetide football in some areas.

Details from an engraving from 1835 showing "La Soule" a football variant played in Normandy and Brittany

The game was played much more violently then the civilized versions we are oh so used to. There were of course two teams, but it was not uncommon to have dozens and even in some cases hundreds of players per side, and rules were almost non-existent, and for this reason in some regions it became known as mob football. Often the game would be played between neighbouring towns, and the rectory balcony was often used as the goal. In these larger games the game ended as soon as the ball entered the goal. Smaller versions were often played as well, in which more reasonable goals were set up, and often the play would continue until a certain score was reached, or there weren't enough players to continue.

There was no rule forbidding touching the ball until much later when football became a common game played at private schools and each school developed its own rule set. In medieval football you could get the ball to the goal by any means necessary. Carrying the ball was often the most common method of transport, but throwing or kicking the ball to teammates was a fairly common practice. In this way medieval football does bear a closer resemblance to American football then it does to association football.

Individual Sports

"A race is not well-run unless you've crossed the finish line knowing that you couldn't have kept going for one more step. If you could have, then you didn't give it everything you had."
Jackie Dugall

Team sports stress the benefits of working together, but individual sports keeps the competitive spirit going but forces contestants to be at their personal best as they play against others on their own merits alone. Many of these games developed into team sports of a sort by adding partners and otherwise altering the rules to allow for additional players, but most were played individually initially.

Individual sports during the medieval age of Europe had a tendency to be geared towards the wealthy. They almost always required specific expensive specialized equipment and/or large areas dedicated to the sport. There are, of course, exceptions to this. Kayles could be played with nothing more than a few sticks gathered, and Quiots was a common pub game using parts scavenged from damaged horse shoes. Games like Golf fit the rule perfectly, it both requires specific specialized equipment that is hard to produce (and thus expensive) and it requires vast amounts of space set aside specifically for the game.

Kayles

Kayles is an ancestor of modern bowling, and it is a game that children have invented and re-invented time and time again throughout the ages. The image on the right is from a 14th century manuscript, so we know it was played back then at least. In Brueghel's Children's games some children are depicted  playing Kayles. Beyond these two sources, the history of Kayles is difficult to trace.

It is played by simply setting up a number of skittles (or pins) and throwing a stick or ball at them to knock down as many as possible. Generally the skittles were set up in a straight line, rather than a triangular pattern that became so popular with bowling.

Kayles would evolve into Skittles which would become a popular pub game throughout England in the 17th century and is still played today. There are now countless varieties of Kayles type games, especially if you consider Bowls, and modern bowling to be part of this family of games, which I do.

Bowls

Bowls, or Boules is a game akin to lawn bowling and is a game that really hasn't changed much over the years. It is related to Bocce and many bowling games.

The earliest evidence of Bowls comes from a 5200 BCE tomb uncovered by Sir Flinders Petrie that has an image of a game which is strikingly similar to Bowls (Pagnoni, 2010). The first written account of bowls comes from William Fitzstephen's description of 12th century London. Fitzstephen describes a game called "in jactu lapidum", which is generally loosely translated to "the casting of stones", but since this is not a direct translation of the phrase, the description seems to fit, and the next entry is about throwing stones for distance it has generally been accepted that Fitzstephen is talking about Bowls ((Translated by unknown) Fitz-William, 1772).

Bowls is played very similar to curling, in that the bowl thrown closest to the target, a jack (small ball or fixed pin), scores, and like curling a bowler who has more than one bowl closer than the next closest bowler scores one point for every bowl closer to the pin than his opponent.

The bowls themselves are not simple round balls, but they are weighted on a "bias", or shaped oddly to have the same effect, that is to have an uneven roll. This adds to the challenge of the game and forces a player to roll the bias. The Italians played, and indeed still do, a similar game to the English Boules variety called Bocce, but the Italian version has no bias on the balls.

Depicts the Legend that Sir Francis Drake was playing bowls when the Spanish Armada arrived in England in 1588. Legend has it Drake insisted on finishing the game before reacting to the arrival of the armada. There is no historical evidence that this event actually took place. (Seymore, 1880)

Golf

Golf is the quintessential Scottish game, and like curling the Scottish people claim the origins of golf belong to Scotland. While there is no direct evidence prove or disprove this belief, there is no real reason to doubt it. While golf like games were being played in various other parts of the world, most notably China, the game that is golf seems a completely Scottish invention.

In 1457 King James II issued an edict banning the sport of golf as it interfered with his subjects practicing archery. In 1471 and again in 1491 King James IV re-enforced this edict calling golf an "unprofitable sport". James IV's edict is a little hypocritical since it is known that he had at least two sets of golf clubs himself (Burnett, 2010).

Golf is modernly considered a more upper class sport, however I tend to believe the sport likely began as a peasant sport. The bans mentioned above seem to lend credibility to this theme as generally bans were for the lower classes than for the gentry and nobility. The equipment is also evidence of this fact.

Modern golf equipment is engineered with a level of science most modern golfers have no understanding of, however golf equipment of medieval Scotland was a totally different matter. Extremely early clubs were entirely wood, and iron got added later. But even then they were using scrap iron for the heads. Early balls were stones that were as round as possible.

As the game grew more popular and the gentry and nobility began to take up the game the equipment got much more complex. Carefully forged heads on the irons, featheries replaced stone balls. The game began to get more of a scientific approach to the equipment.

Featheries were one of the first major breakthroughs in golf equipment. A featherie is a type of golf ball now considered quite archaic. To make one you use two small circles of leather and a strip of leather and sew them together to form a ball shape leaving a small opening which is used to stuff with soaking wet feathers and sew closed. The wet leather will shrink and harden, and the feathers will expand and push against the leather hardening the ball even more. I generally tend to boil the ball after this so that the leather hardens even more. Extant sources state that a top hat worth of feathers is used to fill a single featherie, so you can imagine that you must stuff the ball quite tight. As the ball dries the leather shrinks and hardens and the feathers expand creating quite a solid leather ball. As the ball dries the featherie is hammered into a round shape. Once fully dry several coats of gesso are applied to the ball further hardening the ball and making it the traditional white colour.

Featheries were surprisingly effective. The stitching and seam gap acted in much the same fashion as the dimples do on modern balls. Even after the invention of the gutta percha ball in the 19th century, featheries were still preferred due to their superior action, however the cost made them prohibitive to many golfers and is one of the reasons that golf began to migrate away from being a peasant sport and into a sport of nobility. Once nobility took it over, the game advanced considerably with more and more scientific study being done on equipment to figure out how to make the ball behave exactly the way the players wanted it to.

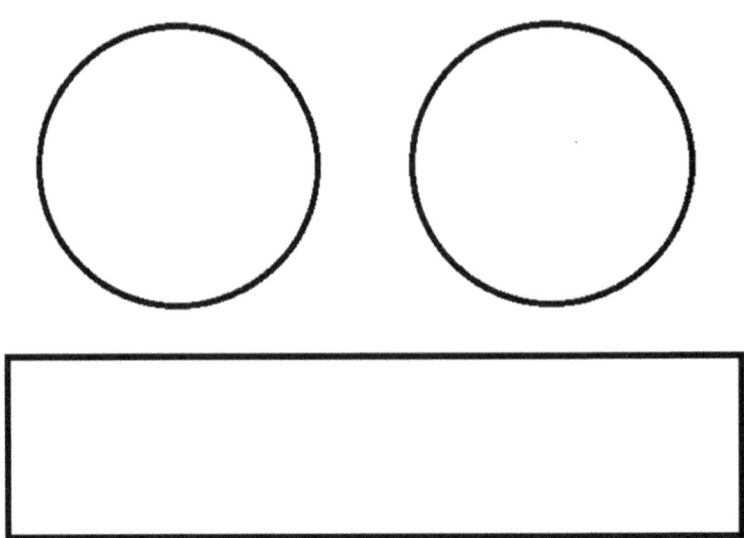

Example of Featherie Pattern

As far as gameplay, the game itself hasn't changed much over time. The basic object of the game is to get the ball into each hole in the fewest strokes possible. The biggest difference between medieval golf and modern golf, besides the equipment, is the number of holes. Eighteen holes was not set as a standard until 1764 when St. Andrews golf course changed their course from eleven holes to nine holes with the option to play the nine from last to first as the back nine.

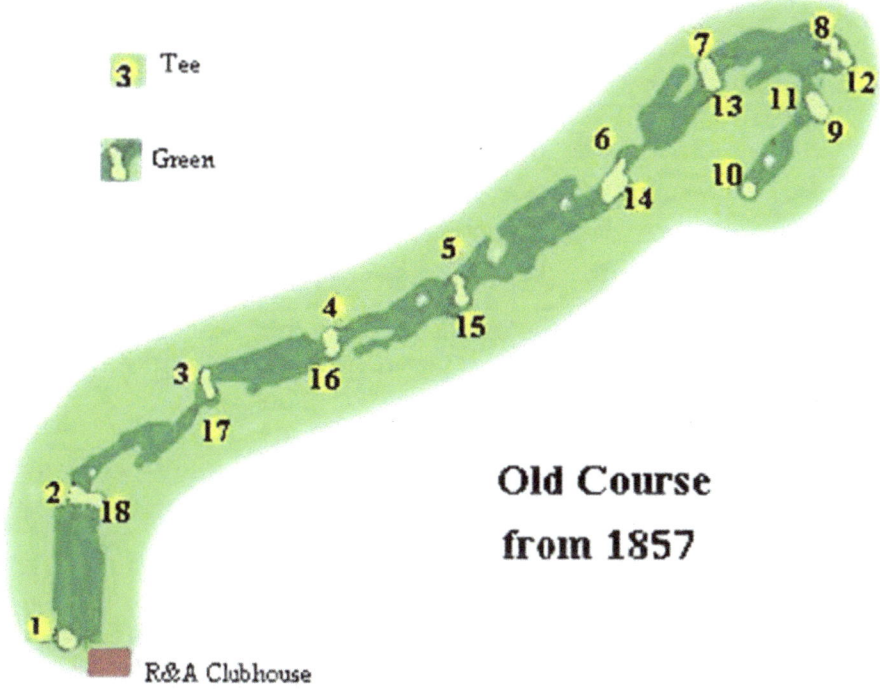

Layout of Old St. Andrews Course, this course is still playable, used with permission from a flyer for St. Andrews Golf Course

The earliest known printed rules of golf come from a competition held at Leith Links by the Honourable Company of Edinburgh Golfers in 1744. While this is clearly outside the scope of medieval ages, there is no evidence that the rules have been altered prior to this in any significant way. The rules as the Honourable Company laid them out were:

1. You must tee your ball within a club's length of the Hole.

2. Your tee must be upon the ground.

3. You are not to change the ball which you strike off the tee

4. You are not to remove stones, bones or any break club, for the sake of playing your ball,

except upon the fair green and that only within a club's length of your ball

5. If your ball comes among water, or any watery filth, you are at liberty to take out your ball and bringing it behind the hazard and teeing it, you may play it with any club and allow your adversary a stroke for so getting your ball.

6. If your balls be found anywhere touching on another, you are to lift the first ball, till you play the last.

7. At holing, you are to play your ball honestly for the hole, and not to play upon your adversary's ball, not lying in your way to the hole.

8. If you should lose your ball, by it's being taken up, or any other way, you are to go back to the spot where you struck last and drop another ball, and allow your adversary a stroke for this misfortune

9. No man at holing his ball is to be allowed to mark his way to the hole with his club or anything else.

10. If a ball be stopped by a person, horse, dog, or anything else, the ball so stopped must be played where it lies.

11. If you draw your club in order to strike and proceed so far in the stroke as to be bringing down your club; if then your club shall break in any way, it is to be accounted a stroke.

12. He whose ball lies farthest from the hole is obliged to play first.

13. Neither trench, ditch nor dyke, made for the preservation of the links, nor the scholar's holes,

or the soldier's lines, shall be accounted a hazard; but the ball is to be taken out, teed and played with any iron club.

(A Pictoral History of American Golf, 1998)

This is an image of Mary Queen of Scots playing golf at St. Andrews. This image appears to be a propaganda piece to discredit Mary. Since golf was seen as a "man's sport" for Mary to be playing it discredits her femininity. This single image is the only evidence this golf game ever took place. (Unknown)

Quoits

Quoits is a traditional English pub game with many similarities to modern horseshoes. It is essentially horseshoes with large metal rings instead of horseshoes. The rings are tossed at pegs in the dirt, closest to the pin scores a point, if the ring actually encircles the peg that is obviously the scoring ring, however if there is more than one ring on the peg only the top ring scores. A different variant has the peg flush with the ground and simply is a target, in this case the rule about the top ring is irrelevant. The pitches could range up to 18 yards long, and the disks can weigh up to 11 pounds. Typically the longer pitches and heavier disks were reserved for the Long Game which had the peg flush with the ground. A shorter version, often referred to as the Northern Game have pitches around 11 yards and disks weighing around 5 pounds. Some claim certain medieval regional versions of the game used disks of up to 23 pounds, though this is hard to verify

In 1388 the Sporting Regulations act condemned the sport and made it illegal. This did nothing to the popularity and Quoit pitches still exist throughout England behind pubs and in peoples' back yards, there is even an indoor version now with scaled down plastic rings. (Masters, 1997)

Tennis

Tennis of the middle ages is almost unrecognizable. It had rackets and a net for sure, but that's where the similarities end. Modern tennis, the tennis most modern folk would recognize as the sport of tennis is more aptly named "lawn tennis" and its medieval counterpart is now known as "real" or "royal" tennis. Lawn tennis really was not developed until the 18th century. (Wilkins, 2002)

Real tennis is an indoor game as opposed to its outdoor lawn tennis cousin. Racket and ball games such as tennis developed in monasteries first, and the layout of a medieval tennis court is definitely reminiscent of this. The court layout is shown in images on the pages at the end of this section.

The equipment in real tennis mainly the same as for lawn tennis, the ball is where the difference is. Modernly those who still play real tennis still used cork balls over the modern latex tennis balls most people are so familiar with. Medievally a leather ball of the same design as a golf feathery (only larger) or stoolball ball was used. Instead of using feathers such as in the feathery, or scraps such as stoolball, the tennis ball was stuffed with hair. Sometimes horse or dog hair, but more often human hair. Barbers could make quite an additional income selling tennis balls from the hair clippings, so much so that there were times that barbers sometimes paid people for their hair. The balls would be stuffed very full so the ball would be as solid as possible.

As with so many medieval sports there were no set definitive rules to playing real tennis (Avedon, et al., 1971). Individual clubs or towns often set their own rules and individual players could of course play by whatever rule standards they both agreed upon. However the game is still played, and since the game never really completely faded out and a continuous history exists it can be presumed that the standard modern rules are fairly close to the rules that would have been used medievally.

The scoring system for real tennis is the same, or at least similar to lawn tennis. Points are awarded in 15's up to a maximum of 60 points, modernly the score goes 15, 30, and 40, game. There is speculation that the 40 was originally 45 and players just shortened it for ease. No one really knows why the point's increment is by 15's, but a common theory holds it has to do with betting. The coin currency in France, where tennis was most popular, was the denier. Laws in the neighbouring Nation of Germany forbade betting on anything with stakes greater than 60 deniers, as it happens one common coin used was worth 15 deniers. Couple these two facts together and you can see a simple betting system using the 15 deniers coin and going to a maximum stake of 60 deniers. (Masters, 1997)

The ball is always served from the service side of the court, and unlike lawn tennis, serving doesn't change between players often. For a serve to be valid the ball must touch the penthouse on the receiving side of the court, the first bounce must be beyond the service line on the hazard end, and the ball must clear the net. Points are won if the other player makes an error such as hitting the net or by a player striking the ball into one of the winning openings (grille, dedans, or winning gallery).

Players change side only when two chases are played, or when a player is at 40 points and one chase is laid. Chases are one of the most complicated aspects of real tennis. A chase is laid when a ball enters any opening other than a scoring opening or if a ball bounces twice on the opposite end from the striker. To win a chase the new server must ensure that the ball has its second bounce closer to the wall than the chase being played. (Oxford University Tennis Club, N/A)

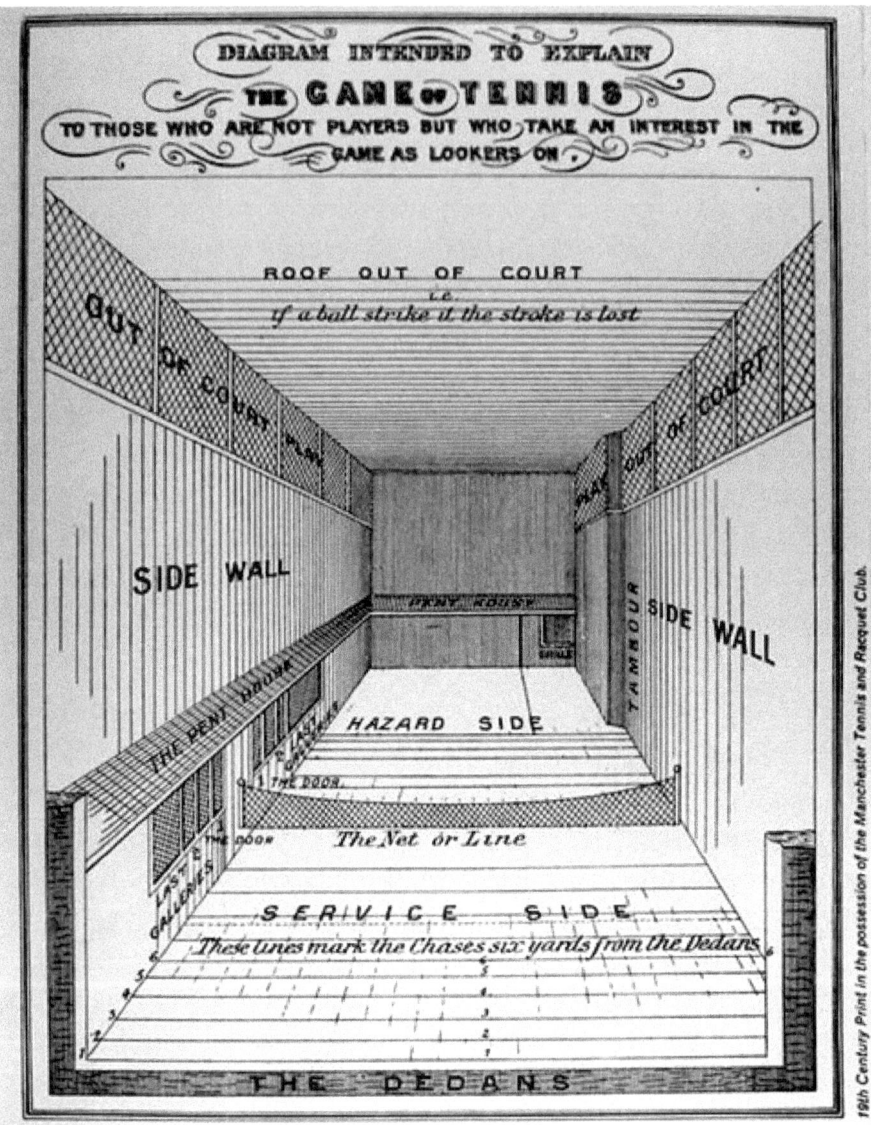

Real Tennis Court Layout

19th Century Print in the possession of the Manchester Tennis and Racquet Club.

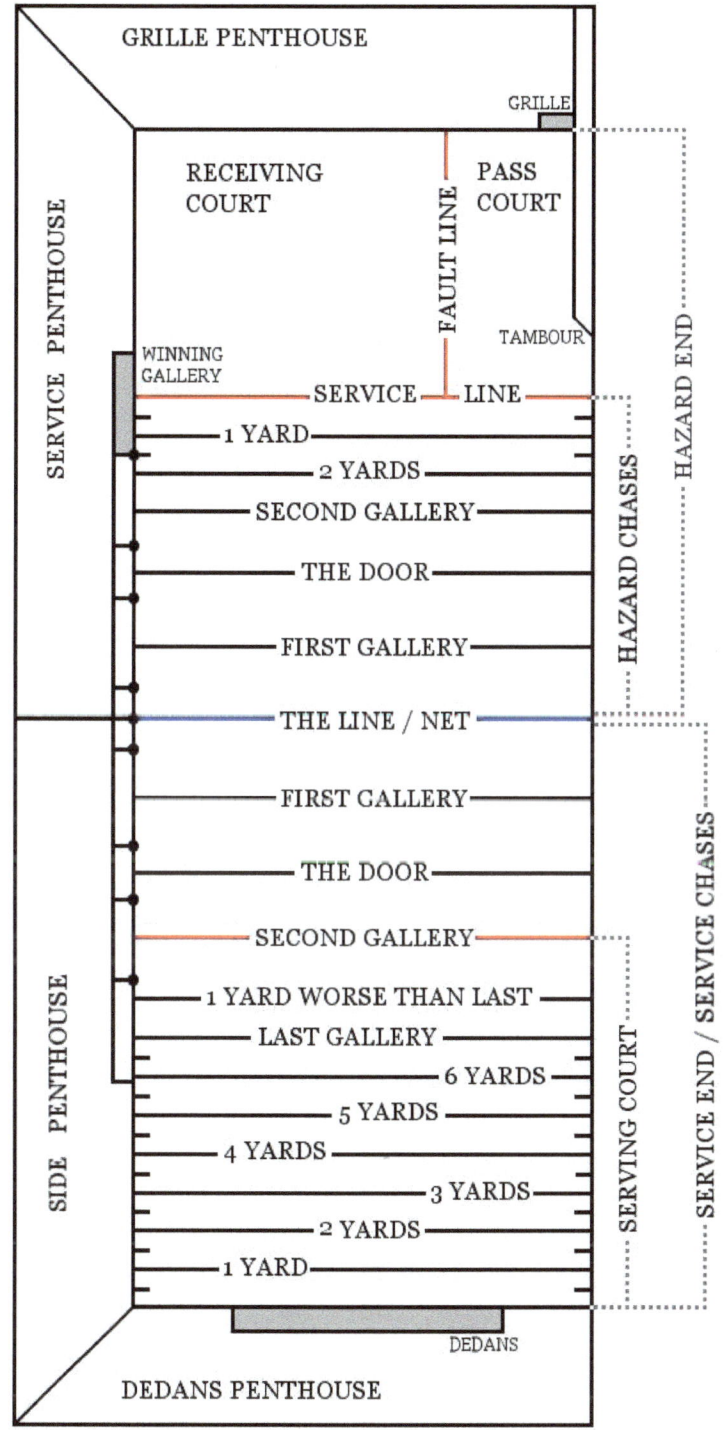

Real Tennis Court Layout From Above

Trucco

Trucco or Trucks is the grandfather of both billiards and croquet, it has often been called Lawn Billiards as well, since it is very similar to medieval billiards. It was a field sport like croquet, instead of mallets spoon like clubs are used, similar to the ones used in Pall Mall.

The game is mentioned in the biography of St. John Berchmans who lived from 1599-1621 (Goldie, 1877). The game is not described in this book however artwork from the early 17th century show the game being played.

There are no limit to the number of players that can play Trucco at the same time, but there are no teams, each player plays for themselves. On the trucco court a free spinning metal hoop is placed and the object is to get your ball through the hoop by hitting the ball with the spoon shaped clubs, much like golf. Doing so scores you three points. Alternately you can hit opponents' balls drawing them away from the hoop and scoring you one point, this is called cannoning. The game ends when one player reaches the agreed upon number of points to win.

Gentlemen Playing Trucco (Artist, Early 17th century)

Pall Mall

Pall Mall is an odd hybrid of golf and croquet with many similarities to Trucco as well. Pall Mall is sometimes referred to as Palle Maille, Pell Mell, Palle-Malle, Palemele, Jeu du Mail, or Palla Maglio depending on region and time period. It is definitely a later period medieval game. The earliest reference to the game can be found in the 1568 Cal. Scot. Papers which state "richt oppinlie at the feildis with the palmall and goif" (Masters, 1997). Pall Mall became a popular enough sport for the name to stick around, Pall Mall Street in London was not just named after the sport, and in fact it used to be a popular Pall Mall court.

PALL-MALL.

In the Diary of Samuel Pepys there is a passage in which Pepys describes seeing a game of Pall Mall played by the Duke of York in St. James Park (Pepys, 2006). Clearly this shows Pall Mall as a sport of the upper class, considering the size of land required for a Pall Mall court it is not surprising that this would be the case.

Joseph Strutt described how the game was played in 1611, "Pale-maille is a game wherein a round box ball is struck with a mallet through a high arch of iron, which he that can do at the fewest blows, or at the number agreed upon, wins. "It is to be observed, that there are two of these arches, that is 'one at either end of the alley.'" The game of mall was a fashionable amusement in the reign of Charles the Second, and the walk in Saint James Park, now called the Mall, received its name from having been appropriated to the purpose of playing at mall, where Charles himself and his courtiers frequently exercised themselves in the practice of this pastime." (Strutt, 1810)

Strutt's explanation falls a little short if you actually wanted to recreate the game, as such I will go into greater detail. Pall Mall is played on fields or alley's as long as 1000 yards with metal hoops suspended several feet off the ground. A wooden boxwood ball slightly larger than a standard croquet ball is used along with wooden mallets and long handled metal spoons. The ball is started from one end of the alley and hit as far as possible towards the hoop at the other end using the wooden mallet. Once the ball is close enough to the hoop the player switches to the spoon to chip it up and into the hoop. The player who gets their ball through the hoop in the fewest strokes wins.

Billiards

Billiards is a well-known game, even to this day, however its history is not so well known. The game can certainly be traced back to 1591 when Edmund Spencer published the poem "Mother Hubbard's Tale" which contains the lines:

> *A thousand wayes he them could entertaine,*
> *With all the thriftles games that may be found;*
> *With mumming and with masking all around,*
> *With dice, with cards, with **billiards** farre unfit*
> *With shuttelcocks, misseeming manlie wit,*
> *With courtizans, and costly riotize,*
> *Whereof still somewhat to his share did rize:*
> (Spencer, 1591)

Robert Littell attributes the invention of Billiards to a French artist by the name of Henrique De Vigne in 1560. (Littell, 1869) However for this to be true the game had to grow in popularity greatly enough in 30 years to be so ingrained into popular culture that Spenser felt comfortable including it in his poem. Others have suggested the game is older than De Vigne's supposed invention, and is simply a table top version of Trucco. (Strutt, 1810)

There is no reason that both versions cannot hold true, it is possible that De Vigne invented the tabletop version of Trucco, a game that was disappearing but still well known, and popularized it as Billiards, the fading popularity of Trucco could explain the rapid growth in the popularity of Billiards since those who enjoyed Trucco but could not afford the space for a Trucco court to play a variant indoors. Plus the fact that it is a perfect game for pubs, keeping the players in the pub, thus drinking more, thus earning the pub owners more money.

Engraving from Charles Cotton's 1674 book, The Compleat Gamester *(Cotton, 1674)*

Medieval Billiards would have retained the hoop to pass through and likely did not have pockets or hazards. Pockets would have had to develop rather quickly though and the 1674 woodcut shown above demonstrates this fact, clearly the hoop still remained in this version, but it quickly faded and a more recognizable billiard table would emerge.

Shovelboard

Shovelboard, modernly called Shuffle Board dates back
to at least the Tudor times in England when it saw quite a
boom in popularity. Henry VIII reportedly lost £9 to Lord
William at Shovelboard, at least according to the Royal Privy
Expenses of 1532. (Masters, 1997)

The medieval version was almost always played on
tabletops, the deck version popular on cruise ships and resorts
is a more modern version dating back to the early 19th century.
Willughby goes into quite a bit of detail in "Book of Games",
in Willughby's version it is coins used as pieces (Willughby,
2003), but other versions use wooden disks, either method is
acceptable.

The simplest form of Shovelboard is to use a long table
and slide disks or coins down the table getting it as close to
the edge without falling over. The player with the disk closest
to the edge scores. Other versions have scoring systems set on
the table. The familiar triangle scoring system of deck versions
of shuffleboard is a modern construct, there is no evidence
that medieval table versions used this.

Feats of Strength

"A man's own hand is most to be trusted."

Viga Glum's Saga

Throughout history man has had a fascination with proving they were better than the others around them, often this results in completions of strength. From how far you could throw a big bolder, to how quickly you could knock a person off their feet, feats of strength were a common way to let off some steam and have some fun.

Wrestling

Wrestling is a common sport of nearly every culture, although different cultures called it different things it was pretty much always the same, a grappling sport in which the goal was to knock down or pin down your opponent.

The Vikings called it *Glima*, and the goal in this wrestling was to knock your opponent off his feet, or pick your opponent up off the ground and throw them to the ground. This sport is mentioned repeatedly in the Sagas and it seems to be a very popular sport (Hurstwic LLC, 1999).

Greeks were particularly fond of wrestling, and Greco-Roman wrestling is still one of the most common forms of wrestling in the world. In ancient Greece, wrestling could actually be your full time profession, it was the most popular sport in most city states in the ancient Greek world. While modern Greco-Roman wrestling is slightly tamer than the wrestling of the ancient Greeks it does retain most aspects of the sport as it was played in Greece (Miller, 2004).

One would expect wrestling to be more a sport of the masses rather than that of nobility, but perhaps one of the most famous wrestling matches of the medieval period is when Henry VIII challenged Francis I of France to a wrestling match at the Field of the Cloth of Gold, a peace summit near Calais in England. Henry was known to be a sportsman and enjoyed all sorts of sports, wrestling amongst them, in a surprise upset Francis I showed that he too was a capable athlete by beating Henry soundly and swiftly. There had been wrestling matches throughout the event between British and French soldiers, with neither country dominating the field, Henry sought to demonstrate British superiority once and for all, but the defeat soured his mood. By all reports the tone of the meeting of monarchs quickly changed after this.

Weightlifting

Weightlifting competitions are, in my opinion, the basest of feats of strength. It is simply a matter of who can lift the heaviest object. Examples of this can be found going back as far as there are records. Galen, a Greek physician from the 2nd century C.E. describes exercises of bearing great weights on the shoulders (Todd, 1995). The Vikings saga also describe a competition in which men lifted heavier and heavier boulders until one was unable to lift one, the man who lifted the heaviest boulder won (Hurstwic LLC, 1999).

Tug of War

Tug of war is a common game to play in large groups. It is impossible to put a specific time period in which the game originated, but it has been around for a very long time. According to *The Notes of Feng*, a Tang dynasty book a game similar to the modern tug of war game was played by soldiers as strength training as early as 8th century B.C.E. (Yu, 2013).

The Viking Sagas also discus tug of wars in a couple of forms. One of the more common forms was for two men to sit on the floor facing each other with their feet touching. Then a rope with loops on either end was held by the loop by each men. The two men would pull until one was pulled over. This game was known as *toga honk* which can be translated as "Tug of War" (Hurstwic LLC, 1999).

Children's Games

"Men do not quit playing because they grow old; they grow old because they quit playing."
Oliver Wendell Holms Jr.

Children are perhaps the most creative inventors of games. They come up with the most fascinating versions of games that adults remember playing as children themselves, often without prompting or teaching the age old games. It's hard to imagine a child that ever lived who did not play tag or hide and go seek, and yet each generation invents a new version of these games, often repeating previous inventions. I remember listing to tales from my daughter as she returned from a hard day of play at the park, regaling me of tales of a new game they created which they were calling "Freeze Tag", she described it as "just like regular tag but when you are tagged you don't become it you just get frozen until someone else unfreezes you". I found this amusing and intriguing, because I remember playing this game myself as a boy, I even remember we named it "Freeze Tag" as well, and yet I don't recall passing such knowledge on to my daughter.

It is of course possible, and even probable that one her friends' parents also played such a game and passed on this knowledge to my daughter. To me it always seemed possible that children instinctively know these games and reinvent them generation after generation. Reliving the exploratory inventions of games created by untold generations before never realizing that they are simply the latest creators of games that have existed as long as humanity has walked the earth, possibly even longer for some games.

This is what fascinates me most about games, how little the old standards change, yet how often they are reinvented. How many variants of Tag can children possibly reproduce, I have no idea, I am not even sure if there is a finite number of versions of Tag possible in this universe.

Baste The Bear

Baste the Bear is a tag like game, where the "it" is called the "bear" and is restrained by a "Keeper". The Keeper is selected by the Bear, the Bear is initially chosen by whatever means the children deem appropriate, drawing of lots works great. The Bear kneels down on the ground with a rope tied about its waist, the Keeper holds the other end of the rope (a length of about five feet is appropriate) and must keep the bear within a circle. The other players use a handkerchief or other bit of cloth as bait to try to hit at the bear run away. Should the Keeper manage to tag on of the other players that player becomes the Bear and chooses his Keeper and the game continues. Alternately should the Bear manage to catch another player around the legs holding him still then that player becomes the Bear just as if the Keeper tagged a player. The Keeper must be careful to keep the bear inside the circle. Should the bear be dragged out of the circle by the keeper then the keeper becomes the bear and the game continues.

Detail From Bruegel's Children's Games

Blind Man's Bluff

Blind Man's Bluff is one of those games that Children just seem to instinctively know, like tag. The history of Blind Man's Bluff is completely lost, no trace of origins seems to be known, although some sources claim to trace it back to the Zhou Dynasty of ancient China.

The game itself is simple enough, it is a tag like game where the person who is "it" is blindfolded. Some versions have any player who is tagged becomes it, while others have players who are tagged removed from the game. In another variant it must identify the person they tag in order for the tag to be valid.

Detail From Bruegel's Children's Games

Hop Scotch

Hopscotch is now pretty much exclusively a children's game, however it didn't start out that way, at least that's what some historians think. There is no hard evidence, but many believe that hopscotch actually started as a military training drill in Rome. Roman soldiers would have to do intricate, and long, hopscotch courts in full armour, sometimes hopping on one leg, or whatever the course demanded. Basically the same way football players often do running drills through tires on the ground. It improves agility and gets you used to operating in armour. While I have found no definitive proof that this was the case it does seem logical, and you could then see it migrating to a children's game as children love to emulate adults, and playing at being a soldier is a pastime even to this day.

There may be no direct evidence that Roman soldiers trained by playing hopscotch, but it can still be demonstrated that hopscotch existed during the Roman Empire. There are hopscotch courts etched into stone all over, but one in particular is scratched into the Forum and clearly can be dated to the height of the Roman Empire. (Newman, 1961) Pilny the Elder who died in 79 C.E. wrote of a game which is definitely related to hopscotch and could possibly be the same game. (Point Park College, Spring 1966)

The name itself comes from the method of making a hopscotch court, scratching it into stone or scotching. It is the same source as the name butterscotch, scoring the candy so it breaks easier. (Hill, 2009)

The game has been passed on from child to child since its beginnings, the design of the courts has changed from generation to generation, but the basic game has remained the same you sketch the court somehow, chalk on pavement is the most common method, the three court designs below are the most common designs.

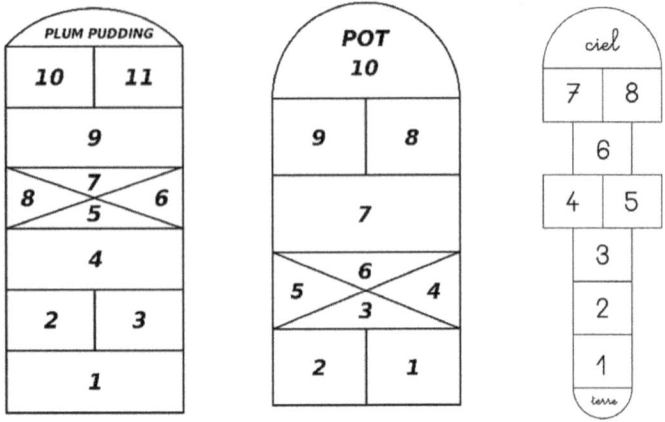

Example of common Hopscotch Court designs from around the world

The game can be played by as many people as you like, but it is best with at least two players. The game begins when the first player throws a stone, or coin or other marker to the #1 square. The player then must hop on all the other squares (except the square the marker is on), the player hops from square to square on one foot only one foot can be on the ground at a time except when there are squares side by side, then both feet must land at the same time. The player must hop to the end turn around (remaining on one foot) then hop back picking up the marker as they pass. If they do this successfully without falling down they continue to the next number on their next turn, if not they remain at the same level and try again next turn. Once the player is done their attempt they hand the marker to the next player who repeats the process. Once a player has done each number square successfully they are the winner.

If you are looking for a more difficult version of hopscotch you could play in armour as the Roman soldiers were said to have, or you could play as some adults did in Medieval England with a friend riding piggyback on your back. (Wilkins, 2002) If carrying extra weight is not your thing vary the design of the court, spiral courts are popular in France in a variant they call Escargot.

Battledore and Shuttlecock

Battledore and shuttlecock is the precursor to modern badminton, in fact badminton's full and proper name is "Badminton House Rules Battledore and Shuttlecock" as it is a variant of battledore and shuttlecock devised at Badminton House in the 1850's and has now become the preferred version of the game (Masters, Battledore and Shuttlecock, 1997). The game has always been particularly popular with children.

Painting dated 1621 Flanders. Girl, about 3 years old, Holding Battledore and Shuttlecock (Somer).

The medieval version did not have nets, it was a simple game of seeing how many times you could hit shuttlecock (birdie) without it touching the ground. The record is apparently held by the Somerset family and was set in 1830, the record is 21,117 hits (Masters, Battledore and Shuttlecock, 1997).

To play battledore and shuttlecock you only need one or more players each with their own racket and one or more shuttlecocks. Simply hit a shuttlecock into the air and play begins. The shuttlecock design was simply a cork with some feathers in it. Rackets were anything from wooden paddles all the way to tennis rackets.

Reproduction battledore and shuttlecock set made by Wendi Dunlap. Photo by Wendi Dunlap, copyright by Wendi Dunlap, all rights reserved, used with permission

*Homemade shuttlecock using a cork and some feathers, made
by the author.*

Hunting Deer in My Lords Park

This is a version of the popular modern children's game of duck, duck, goose but slightly more complex. Everyone stands in a circle facing inwards holding hands spread out as far as possible. The person that is "it" does not stand in the circle but rather walks around outside it and touches someone on the back. The person touched must chase the one that is "it" and follow their exact path, the person that is "it" may weave in and out under other's arms to try and make the chaser lose track of where he went. Should the chaser make a mistake in the path then they are caught and will remain in the circle and the gap they made by chasing is closed. Should the person who is "it" manage to complete the circle and get back to the gap without the chaser catching them than the chaser is caught and remains in the circle and again the circle closes in filling the gap. Should however the chaser catch the person who is "it" they become "it" and the previous person who is "it" takes the chaser's previous spot in the circle. Game continues until there is no more room in the circle. (Willughby, 2003)

Pain Tolerance Games

Children are always quite devious and clever in finding ways to cause each other without it being officially labeled as "Fighting" by the dreaded adults. In fact in researching these medieval pain tolerance games I could not help but notice the similarities between several of them and games I remember playing with my siblings often "slapsies" and "bloody knuckles" came to mind. Of course neither Slapsies nor Bloody Knuckles used a wooden plate to beat on the other as the medieval game Buying of Mustard does, but the concept is very similar, and I am sure results would be as well. Maybe next time I see my brother I'll challenge him to a game of Buying of Mustard to make up for all the games of bloody knuckles we played.

When Francis Willughby wrote his Book of Games it appears that he had a youth, who would have been familiar with this style of gaming, write the entry. Apparently the entire section was written in writing that the 2003 editors felt was probably a juvenile hand, no one really knows who the youth would have been as they are not identified by Willughby in the book anywhere. (Willughby, 2003)

Buying of Mustard

Buying of Mustard is a two player game, for the sake of the explanation we will call the players Player A and Player B. Player A starts out as the seller with a trencher (that is a dinner plate, usually wood or metal) loosely held in his hand. Player A asks player B if he would like to buy any mustard, Player B responds "Is it good". Player A offers Player B a taste. Player B moves forward as if he is going to lick the plate but at some point quickly lashes out grabs the trencher and attempts to slap Player A's hands. If Player B misses he then becomes the seller of mustard and A gets a chance to hit B's hands, if he hits Player A remains the seller and B gets a chance to hit Player A again. (Willughby, 2003)

Cropping of Oats

Cropping of Oats is a two player game, much like Buying of Mustard. One player is the Cropper, the other is the Oat. Both players sit on a narrow bench cross legged. The oat holds his hand palm outward near his ear. The cropper must hit the oats hand and try to knock him off the bench, this is called "cropping the oat". If the cropper succeeds then the oat becomes the cropper. If not he tries again. The player who crops the most oats is the "best cropper" and wins. (Willughby, 2003)

Buying of Bees

Buying of Bees is a game for three players. The three players stand in a line. The middle player places a hat on the ground top down so it forms a bowl, the hat is then called the hive. Then cups his hands before him and asks if the other players will "buy some bees" he must then bend down and put his hands in the hat. The player then will stand back up with his hands at his mouth making a buzzing sound imitating bees. Then he must strike out and hit the other players' ears and attempt to get his hands back in the hat quickly. The other two players must both hit the middle player's ear closest to them before the middle player places his hands back in the hat. If they manage to do this the middle player changes and a new player takes his position, or the game ends. There is no winning or losing really, just an excuse for children to hit each other in a relatively anger free environment. (Willughby, 2003)

A Fool Who Bobbed Thee

This is a game for multiple players, no true limit to the number of players there can be, but it should be more than two, the more players the more difficult the game.

To play A Fool Who Bobbed Thee one player is blindfolded, then one of the players who is not blindfolded boxes the ear of the blindfolded player. The blindfold is removed and the players who was not blindfolded call out "fool, who bobbed thee?" If the player guesses correctly the player who boxed the blindfolded player must be blindfolded and the whole process begins again, if he guesses wrong then he gets blindfolded again and it starts over. (Willughby, 2003)

Appendix A: Images of Tafl Boards

An Alternate Layout for 7X7 Tafl Board
Image ©Damian Walker

Standard Tablut
Image ©Damian Walker

Standard Tawlbwrdd
Image ©Damian Walker

Standard Hnefatafl
Image ©Damian Walker

Appendix B: Images of Speciality Chess Boards

Byzantine Chess
Designed by and available from Guinevere's Games

Four Seasons Chess
Designed by and available from Guinevere's Games

Appendix C: Images of Reproduction Card Decks

Reproduction 15ᵗʰ Century Moorish Deck
Designed by and available from Guinevere's Games

*Swords Suit of the 15th Century Moorish Deck
Designed by and available from Guinevere's Games*

*Cups Suit of the 15th Century Moorish Deck
Designed and available from Guinevere's Games*

The Flemish Hunting Deck

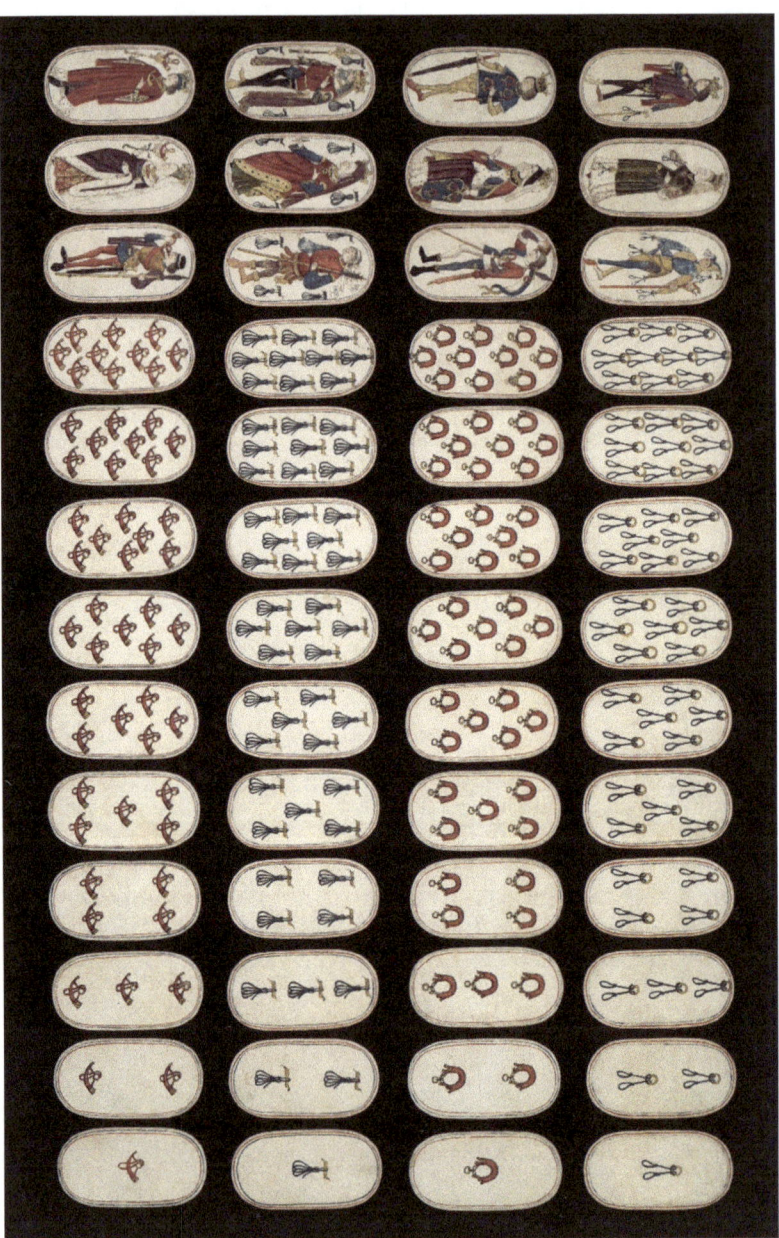

Selected Details

All images from a reproduction deck by Guinevere's Games

King of Nooses

Queen of Nooses

Knave of Nooses

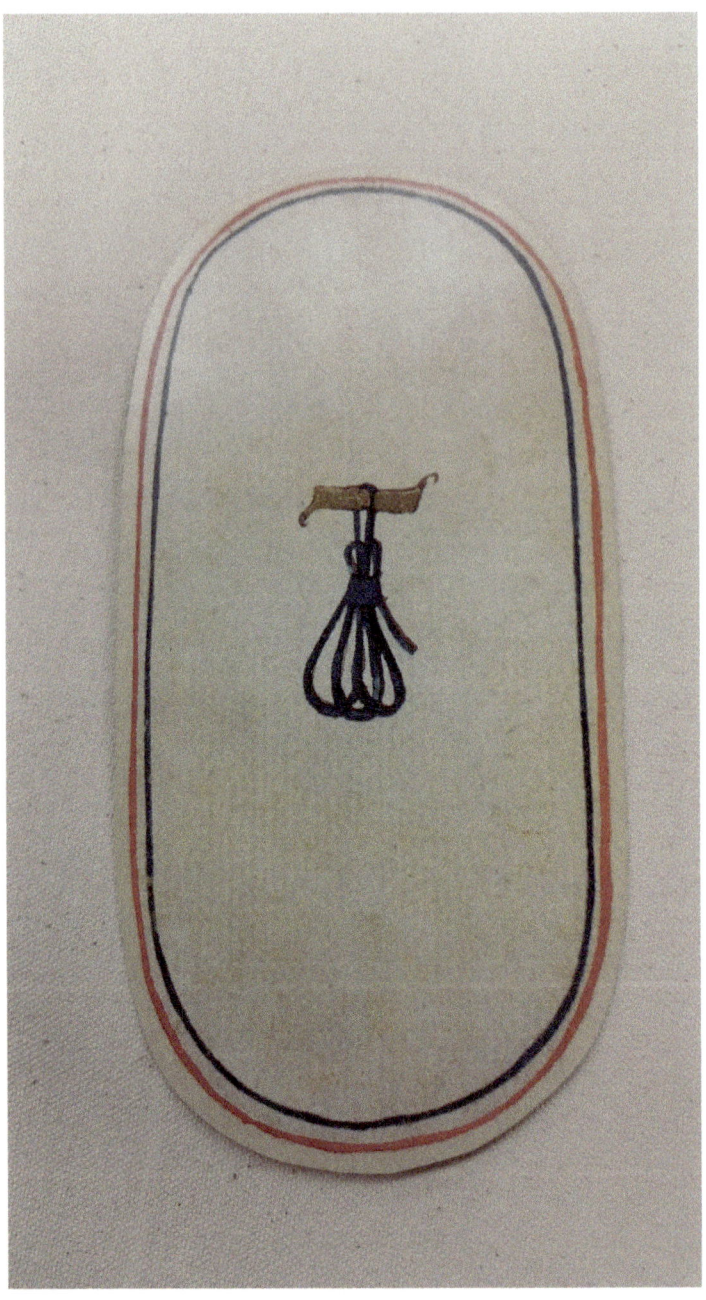

Ace of Nooses

King of Tethers

Queen of Tethers

Knave of Tethers

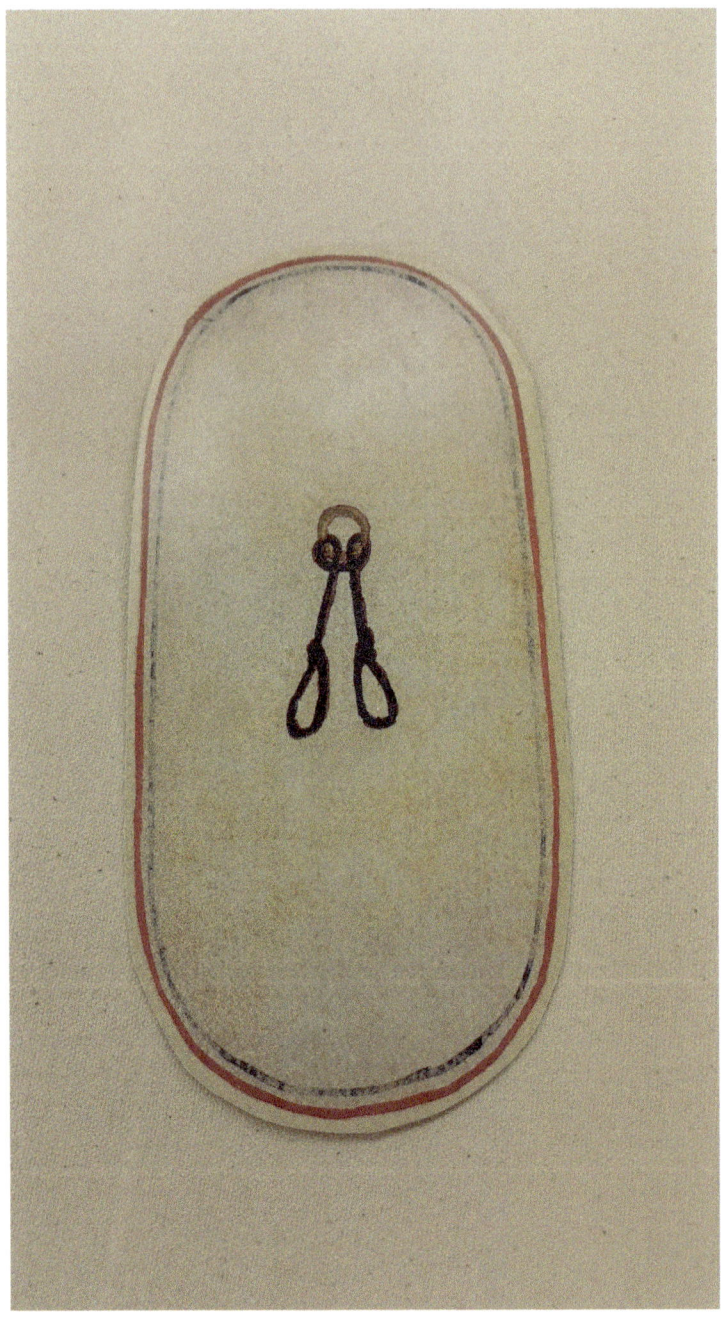

Ace of Tethers

King of Horns

Queen of Horns

Knave of Horns

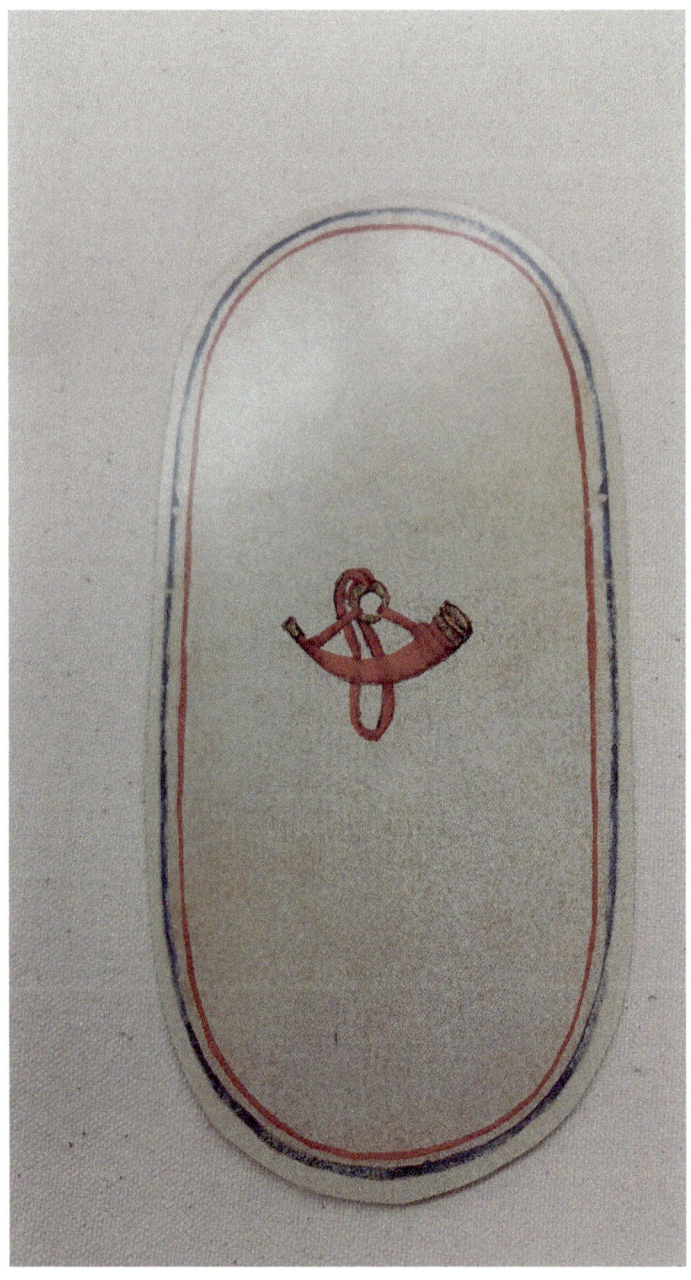

Ace of Horns

King of Collars

Queen of Collars

Knave of Collars

Ace of Collars

Appendix D: List of Useful Websites

As with all information on the Internet it constantly changes, I cannot guarantee the quality of the information on these pages, or even that the pages still exist when you are reading this. But at the time of publication these are some of the best websites focusing on medieval games:

MacGregor Historical Games - http://historicgames.com/

Hnefatafl – The Game of the Vikings - http://tafl.cyningstan.org.uk/

Games Guild of Ealdormere – http://gamesguildofealdormere.blogspot.ca

Avacal Games Guild -

http://cuallaidh.hubpages.com/hub/avacal-games-guild

Rules to Period Games - http://jducoeur.org/game-hist/game-rules.html

Stoolball: a medieval baseball game - http://slumberland.org/sca/articles/stoolball.html

Dagonell's Medieval Games - http://www-cs.canisius.edu/~salley/SCA/Games/

Online Guide to Traditional Games - http://www.tradgames.org.uk/

Elliott Avedon Virtual Museum of Games - http://www.gamesmuseum.uwaterloo.ca/

Guinevere's Games - https://www.guineveresgames.ca/

Medieval and Renaissance Games Homepage - https://www.querki.net/u/jducoeur/period-games/#period-games

Bibliography

2007. *Lodi Curling Club.* [Online] 2007. http://www.lodicurling.org/the-game/.

(Translated by unknown) Fitz-William, Stephen. 1772. *Fitz-Stephen's Description of the City of London, Newly Translated from The Original Latin, with Necessary Comentary.* 1772.

1998. *A Pictoral History of American Golf.* s.l. : Willow Creek Press, 1998.

Artist, Unknown. Early 17th century. *Getlemen Playing Trucco.* Sotheby's Catalogue #L07123, Important British Paintings 1500-1850 22 November 2007, s.l. : Early 17th century.

Avedon, Elliott M. and Sutton-Smith, Brian. 1971. *The Study of Games.* London : John Wiley & Sons, 1971.

Bell, Robert Charles. 1979. *Board and table games from many civilizations Volume I.* New York : Dover, 1979.

—. 1979. *Discovering Backgammon.* New York : Shire Publications, 1979.

Block, David. 2006. *Baseball Before We Knew It.* s.l. : Bison Books, 2006.

Burnett, Allan. 2010. Slicing into History. *Discover NLS:*

The Magazine of the National Library of Scotland. Summer 2010.

Chaucer, Geoffrey. 1475. *Canterbury Tales.* 1475.

Coeur, Justin du. 1995. Game Report: Picket. *Medieval & Renaissance Games Home Page.* [Online] 30 November 1995. [Cited: 28 October 2014.] http://jducoeur.com/game-hist/game-recon-picket.html.

—. **2003.** Game Report: Primero. [Online] 26 October 2003. [Cited: 10 December 2014.] http://jducoeur.com/game-hist/game-recon-primero.html.

Cotton, Charles. 1674. *The Compleat Gamester.* s.l. : Routledge, 1674.

Dunlap, Wendi. 2006. Stool ball: a medieval baseball game. [Online] 2006. http://slumberland.org/sca/articles/stoolball.html.

Eales, Richard. 2007. Changing Cultures: The Reception of Chess into Western Europe in the Middle Ages. [book auth.] I.L. Finkel. *Ancient Board Games in Perspective: Papers from the 1990 British Museum colloquium, with additional contributions.* 2007.

Ekblom, Björn. 1994. *Handbook of sports medicine and science. Football.* 1994.

Flötner, Peter. *Playing Cards.* British Museum, London : s.n.

Fontananera, Signore Giovanni. 1993. Period Pasteboard Pastimes. *Tournaments Illustrated.* 1993, 106.

From Circle and Square to the Image of the World: A Possible Interpretation for Some Petroglyphs of Merels Boards. **Berger, Friedrich. 2004.** 2004, Rock Art Research Vol. 21 Number 1, pp. 11-25.

Ghistelles Hours. Library of the Walters Art Museum, s.l. : s.n.

Goldie, Francis. 1877. *The life of blessed John Berchmans.* s.l. : Burns and Oates, 1877.

Golladay, Sonja Musser. 2003. *Alfonso X's Book of Games.* 2003.

—. **2007.** *Los Libros De Acedrex Dados E Tablas: Historical, Artistic and Metaphysical Dimensions of Alphonso X's Book of Games.* Arizona : The University of Arizona, 2007.

Golombek, Harry. 1976. *Chess A History.* New York : G.P. Putnam's Sons, 1976.

Gordon, Eric Valentine. 1981. *An Introduction to Old Norse.* s.l. : Oxford University Press, 1981.

Gross, Paul. 2002. *Men With Brooms.* 2002.

Gunther, William. 2013. *Cribbage Board.* [CC-BY-SA-3.0 (http://creativecommons.org/licenses/by-sa/3.0)], via Wikimedia Commons, s.l. : 2013.

Henderson, Robert W. 1947. *Ball, Bat and Bishop: The Origins of Ball Games.* 1947.

Hill, Nancy S. 2009. *The One Year Did You Know Devotions 2.* s.l. : Tyndale Kids, 2009.

Holme, Randle. 1688. *The Academy of Armory.* 1688.

Hurstwic LLC. 2006. Hurstwic. *Knattleikr.* [Online] Hurstwic LLC, 2006. http://www.hurstwic.org/history/articles/daily_living/text/knattleikr.htm.

—. **1999.** Hurstwic. *Games and Sports in the Viking Age.* [Online] Hurstwic LLC, 1999. [Cited: 24 November 2014.] http://www.hurstwic.org/history/articles/daily_living/text/games_and_sports.htm.

Jacoby, Oswald and Crawford, John R. 2000. History of Backgammon. *Bacgammon Galore!* [Online] 2000. [Cited: 26 June 2013.]

http://www.bkgm.com/articles/JacobyCrawford/History/.

Jacoby, Oswald and Crawford, John R. 1970. History of Backgammon. *Backgammon Galore!* [Online] April 1970. http://www.bkgm.com/articles/JacobyCrawford/History/part2.html.

Knutson, C. 2010. *Early Games of Dice.* Minneapolis : Rose & Pentagram Design, 2010.

Littell, Robert S. 1869. *Littel's Living Age Volume 100.* 1869.

Mark, Michael. 2007. The Beginnings of Chess. [book auth.] I.L. Finkle. *Ancient Board Games in Perspective: Papers from the 1990 British Museum colloquium, with additional contributions.* 2007.

Masters, James. 1997. Battledore and Shuttlecock. *Online Guide to Traditional Games.* [Online] 1997. [Cited: 29 September 2011.] http://www.tradgames.org.uk/games/Battledore-Shuttlecock.htm.

—. **1997.** Cribbage. *The Online Guide to Traditional Games.* [Online] 1997. http://www.tradgames.org.uk/games/Cribbage.htm.

—. **1997.** Golf, Kolf, Colf and Pall Mall. *The Online Guide to Traditional Games.* [Online] 1997. http://www.tradgames.org.uk/games/Golf.htm.

—. **1997.** Quoits - History and Useful Information. *The Online Guide to Traditional Games.* [Online] 1997. http://www.tradgames.org.uk/games/Quoits.htm.

—. **1997.** Shut the Box - History and Useful Information. *The Online Guide to Traditional Games.* [Online] 1997. [Cited: 26 June 2013.] http://www.tradgames.org.uk/games/Shut-The-Box.htm.

—. **1997.** Tennis. *The Online Guide to Traditional Games.*

[Online] 1997.
http://www.tradgames.org.uk/games/Tennis.htm.

—. **1997.** The Shovel-Board Family - History and Useful Information. *Online Guide to Traditional Games.* [Online] 1997. http://www.tradgames.org.uk/games/ShovelBoard.htm.

Mebben, Peter. Rithmomachia, the Philosophers' Game. [Online] http://jducoeur.org/game-hist/mebben.ryth.html.

Miller, Christopher. 2004. *Submission Fighting and the Rules of Ancient Greek Wrestling.* s.l. : First published at Judoinfo.com, 2004.

Miller, Gretchen. To Play Piquet. [Online] [Cited: 28 October 2014.]
http://www.cs.cmu.edu/afs/andrew/org/Medieval/www/src/contributed/grm/games/piquet.html.

Murray, H.J.R. 1913. *A History Of Chess.* s.l. : Oxford University Press, 1913.

Nelson, Walter. 2007. *The Merry Gamester.* Reseda : s.n., 2007.

Newman, Paul B. 1961. *Daily Life in the Middle Ages.* s.l. : McFarland & Company, 1961.

O'Rahilly, Cecile. 1967. *Táin Bó Cuailnge from the Book of Leinster.* 1967.

Oxford University Tennis Club. N/A. An Outline of the Rules of Real Tennis. *Oxford University Tennis Club.* [Online] N/A. http://www.outc.org.uk/realtennisrules.html.

Pagnoni, Mario. 2010. *The Joy of Bocce 3rd Edition.* s.l. : AuthorHouse , 2010.

Parlett, David. 1992. *A Dictionary of Card Games.* Oxford : Oxford University Press, 1992.

—. **2013.** Laugh and Lie Down. *Davidparlette.co.uk.*

[Online] February 2013.
http://www.davidparlett.co.uk/histocs/laughand.html.

—. **1996.** *Oxford Dictionary of Card Games.* s.l. : Oxford
University Press, 1996.

Pepys, Samuel. 2006. *The Diary of Samuel Pepys 1661.*
[ed.] Henry B. Wheatly. 2006.

Peterson, Neil. 2001. *Hnefatafl: An Experimental
Reconstruction.* 2001.

Pieter Bruegel, the Elder, 1560. *KINDERSPIELE
(Childern's Games).*

Point Park College. Spring 1966. Pennsylvania
Folklore Society. *Keystone folklore quarterly.* Spring 1966, Vol.
Volume 11.

Rabelais, Francois. 1894. *Gargantua and his son
Pantagruel.* Derby : Moray Press, 1894.

Routledge, E. 1881. *Every boy's book: a complete
encyclopædia of sports and amusements.* 1881.

Sackson, Sid. 1999. *The Book of Classic Board Games.* s.l. :
Klutz, 1999.

Seymore, John. 1880. *The Armada in Sight.* Art Gallery
of New South Wales Sydney, New South Wales, Australia :
1880.

Smith, James Edward. 1811. *Lachesis Lapponica, or a
Tour in Lapland.* London : White and Chochrane, Horace's
Head, 1811.

Somer, Paul Van. *Portrait of a Girl Holding a Battledor
and Shuttlecock.* 1621 : s.n.

Spencer, Edumund. 1591. *Complaints.* 1591.

Stirling Stone. Stirling Smith Art Gallery and Museum,
s.l. : s.n.

Stoolball England. Starter Stoolball. *Stoolball England.* [Online] http://www.stoolball.org.uk/rules/starter-stoolball/.

Strutt, Joseph. 1810. *The Sports and Pastimes of the People of England: Including the Rural and Domestic Recreations, May-Games, Mummeries, Pageants, Processions, and Pompus Spectacles.* 1810.

Suzuki, Jeff A. 1994. Primero: A Renaissance Cardgame. [Online] 1994. [Cited: 10 December 2014.] http://math.bu.edu/INDIVIDUAL/jeffs/primero.html.

Thibault, Daniel U. Game Cabinet. *Rithmomachia.* [Online] http://www.gamecabinet.com/rules/Rithmomachia.html.

Thordarson, Sveinbjorn. *Icelandic Saga Database.* [Online] [Cited: 25 November 2014.] http://www.sagadb.org.

Todd, Jan. 1995. From Milo to Milo: A History of Barbells, Dumbbells, and Indian Clubs. *Iron Game History.* 1995, Vol. 3, 6.

University of Waterloo. 2010. Dice Games. *Elliott Avedon Virtual Museum of Games.* [Online] 11 February 2010. [Cited: 25 June 2013.] http://gamesmuseum.uwaterloo.ca/VirtualExhibits/Alfonso/dice.html.

—. 2010. Dreidel - Put & Take - Teetotum. *Elliott Avedon Virtual Museum of Games.* [Online] 24 March 2010. [Cited: 25 June 2013.] http://gamesmuseum.uwaterloo.ca/VirtualExhibits/Tablegames/Dreidel/.

Unknown. 2010. Gluckhaus. *Cunnan.* [Online] 22 July 2010. [Cited: 25 July 2013.] http://cunnan.sca.org.au/wiki/Gluckhaus.

Unknown, "The Illustrated London News". *Mary*

Queen of Scotts Playing Golf at St. Andrews. National Library of Scotland ref. NJ.677, s.l. : s.n.

Voss, Ernst. 1930. Karnoeffelspiel, A German Card Game of the Sixteenth Century. *Transactions of the Wisconsin Academy of Sciences, Arts and Letters.* 1930, Vol. XXV.

Wilkins, Sally. 2002. *Sports and Games of Medieval Cultures.* London : Greenwood Press, 2002.

—. **2002.** *Sports and Games of Medieval Cultures.* London : Greenwood Press, 2002.

Willughby, Francis. 2003. *Francis Willughby's Book of Games: A seventeenth-Century Treatise on Sports, Games and Pastimes.* [ed.] Jeffrey L. Forgeng, Dorothy Johnston David Cram. s.l. : Ashgate, 2003.

Yu, Junli. 2013. *Research on the Customs of festival sports entertainment in Tang Dynasty from Angles of Poems and Proses.* s.l. : International Academic Workshop on Social Science, 2013.

Index

Lightning Source UK Ltd.
Milton Keynes UK
UKHW050820270519
343376UK00008B/404/P